The High-Impact Middle Manager

Powerful Strategies to Thrive in the Middle

Lisa Haneberg

ASTD
PRESS

Alexandria, Virginia

ASTD Press is an internationally renowned source of insightful and practical information on workplace learning and performance topics, including training basics, evaluation and return-on-investment, instructional systems development, e-learning, leadership, and career development. Visit our website at www.astd.org.

Ordering information: Books published by ASTD Press can be purchased by visiting ASTD's website at store.astd.org or by calling 800.628.2783 or 703.683.8100.

Library of Congress Control Number: 2009925589

ISBN-10: 1-56286-697-4
ISBN-13: 978-1-56286-697-6

ASTD Press Editorial Staff:
Director of Content: Dean Smith
Manager, ASTD Press: Jacqueline Edlund-Braun
Senior Associate Editor: Tora Estep
Senior Associate Editor: Justin Brusino
Editorial Assistant: Victoria DeVaux

Copyeditor: Alfred Imhoff
Indexer: April Michelle Davis
Proofreader: Kris Patenaude
Interior Design and Production: Kathleen Schaner
Cover Design: Steve Fife
Cover Art: Digital Vision

Printed by Versa Press, Inc., East Peoria, IL

To all the corporate superheroes out there,
leading from the middle, and making an impact
while swallowing a fire hose dose of to-do list items.

Contents

Foreword

I t has been 13 years since *Flight of the Buffalo: Soaring to Excellence, Learning to Let Employees Lead*, the book that Jim Belasco and I wrote together, was published. These 13 years have provided a lot of time to study and reflect on the ideas and principles espoused in that book. An active career as the CEO of a large, rapidly growing company and as a coach to leaders of other companies has provided many opportunities to test and refine my beliefs about what it takes to create an organization that continually performs at a high level.

We know that people are what make the difference in an organization. Their performance determines the performance of the organization. Great people make great companies. But what makes people great? That is what my book was about—helping leaders to create an environment that helps and encourages rising to greatness. The question I have been pondering since that book is a more difficult one: What keeps them great over a period of time?

What I have found is that greatness doesn't just happen. People and organizations learn how to become great through constant effort. The few people who maintain their greatness over many years have learned to focus on becoming great—not on being great. It is that focus on becoming that keeps people learning and growing even though their performance is already at an extraordinary level.

Tiger Woods didn't start out great. He learned how to become great through many years of training both his mind and his body. This resulted in a great victory at the Masters, where he won with a record margin. Shortly after that victory, he realized that he had flaws in his swing that would prevent him from reaching his goal of being the greatest golfer in history. He spent the greater part of a year removing those flaws and has since played at a much higher level. I suspect that even now he is working on ways to once more widen the gap between him and his competitors.

Lisa Haneberg is very much like Tiger. She is driven to continuously learn and improve her effectiveness. We first met while working together to create high-performing leadership teams at a division of the Mead Paper Company. Her work there was outside the ordinary for a human resources person, and it had a huge impact on her company. This work served as a springboard for her learning about performance that she has doggedly pursued to this day. *The High-Impact Middle Manager* is a result of that work.

The High-Impact Middle Management System is a very important contribution to the study of organizational effectiveness because it focuses on the people who are the key to any organization's performance—the people in the middle. These are the people whose efforts determine the success of any endeavor. Leaders can design wonderful strategies, but the success of the organization resides in the execution of those strategies. The people in the middle are the ones who make it work. Based on all the companies I've seen, including my own, I'll take an average strategy that is extremely well executed over a great strategy with mediocre execution every time. That is why we spend a substantial amount of our development efforts on this group of individuals at my company. We know who drives our performance.

That is why this book is so valuable. When Lisa first asked me to write this foreword, she sent me the book to read. I found a number of excellent development concepts in it, so I gave it to our personnel development department. They found the book very helpful and have incorporated a number of concepts into the work at Johnsonville Sausage. We think it will be very helpful in our efforts to become the best sausage company in the world. I am sure you will also find value in it.

Ralph C. Stayer
CEO and owner, Johnsonville Sausage, Inc.

Acknowledgments

The High-Impact Middle Management System has developed over many years and with the participation and cooperation of hundreds of middle managers. My thanks to all the managers with whom I have had the honor to work at Black & Decker, Mead Paper, Intel, Amazon .com, and Cruise West. Special thanks go to the managers with whom I worked very closely, including Jim Booth, Dave Borden, Johna Campbell, Melanie Cole, Jerre Fuqua, Dave Giblin, Jeff Hedges, Barry Kelly, Jeff Krida, Kate Mulqueen, John Pemberton, Timo Shaw, Karin Thompson, John Underwood, Martha Wharton, and Denny Wormington. You have shaped my thinking and this book. I am also grateful to Ralph Stayer, the CEO of Johnsonville Foods, for his inspiration, coaching, and support over the past 13 years and for writing the foreword. This book could not have become a reality without these and many other people who believed in the book and me. I am grateful to them all.

Finally, I thank my wonderful husband, Bill, who selflessly gave his time and support to me during the book's creation.

....

Middle Management— Magic or Mayhem?

In any organization, there are two kinds of middle managers. There are those who get the work done but never think beyond what needs to be completed in the short term. They rush from one task to another, never quite recognizing which is most important to their company's larger objectives. Though they may work hard and have good intentions, they fail to see the big picture and, thus, add little value to their organization or the functions they manage. Then there are high-impact middle managers. These managers see the big picture. They know how to manage operational practices and execute tactical goals to support strategic initiatives. They add value to their organization and thus elevate their position from that of an intermediary to key player.

There is an almost magical synergy in a work environment when high-impact middle managers operate at peak efficiency. Their questions are timely and on target; their ideas are provocative in ways that help move the work forward. They know how to think strategically. Transitions from one task to the next seem choreographed. As they walk through the office, their demeanor is calm but they have a sense of urgency. Busy, focused, and driven, these managers produce results and imbue the workplace with energy. Those who watch these managers may feel motivated or intimidated—but they are not unaffected.

Although their days are full, they have more time at their disposal than other middle managers who produce less. That's because these effective middle managers use tiny pockets of time to accomplish big things. They plan well and anticipate whatever is coming their way. When they do make a mistake, they quickly solve the problem and learn from the experience. These middle managers are effective because they understand what they need to do, methodically do those things, and adjust quickly and proactively when barriers pop up or conditions change.

Unfortunately, most middle managers have never experienced this kind of productivity. They spend their days trying to catch up, never mind moving ahead. Barriers and challenges bring their productivity to a grinding halt. They focus on the urgent rather than the important. Disconnected by a lack of communication with their peers and managers, their work is no longer aligned to achieve results, and team members lose sight of how their work influences the organization or why it even matters. Results suffer because the middle manager and his or her team are not set up to deliver them.

Nothing is more heartbreaking than seeing smart, hardworking, and well-meaning managers fail. But in today's ever-changing and competitive work environment, it happens all too often. Success is most difficult for middle managers, because their role is more complicated and challenging than the roles of either frontline supervisors or senior executives. Even so, middle managers can experience peak performance with the right guidance, development, and support. To do so, they need to learn the craft of middle management and overcome several challenges that can wreck their capacity to perform.

A great middle manager—referred to in this book as a high-impact middle manager—is an individual who makes substantial qualitative and quantitative contributions to his or her organization and moves work forward with velocity—speed and direction. The high-impact middle manager can straddle several planning periods to address the needs of today, this week, this month, this year, and the next few years. He or she understands the difficult and complex nature of his or her role and feels energized by being the conduit between corporate thought, action, and results. High-impact middle managers "get it." They know that their job is the most exciting one for those who relish being in the thick of it.

This book offers a vision of high-impact middle management and a system for achieving this superior level of performance. The High-Impact Middle Management System provides busy middle managers with an integrated set of practices and techniques that maximize results and success. It is a distinct system because it addresses corporate execution and success from the perspective of middle management, recognizes that middle management is the engine for corporate results, and offers regimens and practices to ensure performance.

Who Is a Middle Manager?

Depending on the size of the company, middle managers may hold the title of vice president, director, or manager. Middle management positions are responsible leadership posts typically two to seven layers below the president. They may have other supervisors or managers reporting to them and are responsible for managing at least one function within the company. Middle managers are not CEOs, but they are high enough on the corporate ladder that they are expected to understand and take part in creating business plans, budgets, and other planning documents.

The Motivation for This Book

Middle managers have a more direct impact on business results than any other layer of an organization; it is vital, therefore, that they receive the resources and development they need. Sadly, there are few books or training programs targeted to meet the unique needs of middle managers. This is unacceptable and a serious concern, because businesses suffer when middle managers do not know what to do. As the glue that connects corporate strategy to work productivity, middle managers can either enable or impede corporate accomplishments.

The observations, tools, and suggestions that make up the High-Impact Middle Management System—as they have been developed and perfected over many years—have helped many middle managers do their jobs better. This book, which distills this system, is one of the few that explains and illustrates successful middle management practices and tools. Its goal is thus to share this system of management in a way that is clear and easy to implement. Middle managers who incorporate this system into their daily practices will receive a payoff of improved management skills, better results, and increased promotability. If you are a middle manager, implementing the system detailed in the pages that follow will enable you to enjoy your job more fully, see better results, and experience peak performance from yourself and your team.

How the Book Is Organized

This book offers a comprehensive look at the challenges and opportunities that middle managers face in today's business climate. Each part addresses a dimension, or layer, of the middle manager's job. Part I is focused on helping you to fully understand and appreciate your role as a middle manager. Part II offers techniques for planning and measuring results and performance. Part III looks at how structure and time can enable or hinder your success and defines practices that will help you improve your productivity. Performance optimization and leadership are at the heart of part IV. And in part V, you will learn how to fully utilize the techniques explained in this book.

Although the information in each part and chapter can be read and applied separately, you will find the techniques to be complementary and additive. The more you try and use them, the greater your results will be. Please enjoy the book's chapters in the order that best addresses your needs; however, I do recommend reading part I before the other parts, because it explains the foundations and assumptions of the High-Impact Middle Management System.

A Powerful Force
for Executing Results

Chapter 1

The High-Impact Middle Management System

The numbers were in. Black & Decker had regained the market share it had lost over the past several years—and then some. The company's new DeWalt line of power tools had made it to the marketplace in record time and had received rave reviews. It was a great lineup. The tools represented cutting-edge technology, and they were beautifully designed and expertly packaged. Cross-functional international product development teams had worked tirelessly on the DeWalt line design, development, and launch for more than two years. And now their hard work had really paid off for Black & Decker, giving it the boost in the marketplace that it sorely needed. Everyone involved in the DeWalt launch knew they had been part of something special.

It would be hard to argue that the DeWalt vision and strategy for producing a superior line of tools for the serious do-it-yourselfer and the professional were not brilliant; they set the stage for the right work to happen. The inspiring strategy got the team started, but what made the DeWalt plan's execution so successful was the quality of Black & Decker's middle managers. In the end, it was high-impact middle managers who produced breakthrough results and put Black & Decker back on the map as a major player in the competitive do-it-yourself power tool market. How did they do it?

- They were extraordinarily good project managers.
- They had an uncompromising attitude about hiring only the best for the DeWalt team.
- They practiced effective cross-functional and international communication.
- They established an environment that encouraged creativity and innovation.
- They planned well and made sure that priorities were crystal clear.
- They communicated the vision of the senior executives with passion and clarity.

Black & Decker's team of high-impact middle managers did outstanding work and made a significant contribution to a companywide achievement. That is high-impact middle management in action.

What Middle Managers Do

Middle managers are the fundamental link joining an organization's strategies to the people and projects needed to produce results. They are the folks in the middle who see and manage how various parts of the enterprise work. It's a big and often underestimated responsibility. Figure 1-1 shows what the typical middle manager's role might look like. In the top portion of the figure, various concerns converge and compete for a middle manager's time and attention. These concerns include a broad range of tasks such as planning, goal setting, performance management, problem solving, process improvement, relationship building, analysis, communication updates, budgeting, and decision making. Barriers and mucky-muck (see chapter 6) can block these items from getting the time and consideration they deserve.

The funnel represents the distillation process that middle managers must use to decide how they will spend time and complete their work. Middle managers are like a corporate funnel, interpreting and translating strategies, needs, and choices so their teams can perform. They practice

Figure 1-1. The Typical Middle Manager's Role

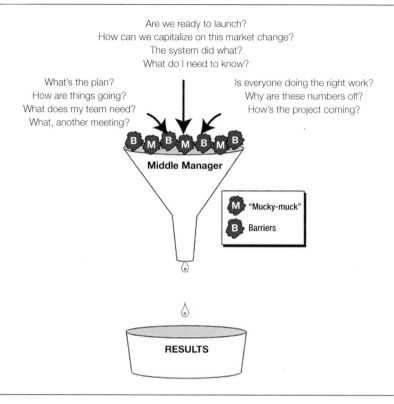

techniques and make decisions that influence results. Ineffective work practices and a preponderance of barriers can combine to slow output to a trickle.

Figure 1-2 shows what results can look like when managers use the High-Impact Middle Management System. The results are much better! High-impact middle management helps middle managers deal with daily tasks and strategic demands while providing tools to reduce barriers to productivity. Middle management areas of concern that high-impact middle management addresses include

- paradigms that best serve execution and results
- fostering collaboration to improve results and efficiency
- determining team performance
- goal setting for peak performance

Figure 1-2. A Middle Manager Using High-Impact Middle Management Techniques

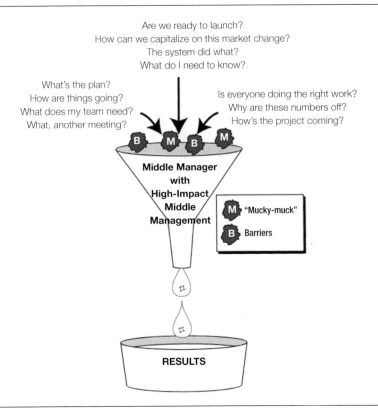

- dealing with daily obstacles to results
- removing factors that limit throughput
- time management
- process alignment techniques
- performance management techniques
- skills for coaching others
- using the High-Impact Middle Management System to improve results
- honing middle management skills to build your career.

By using high-impact middle management, you will save time and resources by focusing your efforts in areas where they will have the greatest impact. In addition, this book presents a number of techniques that can facilitate breakthroughs—those quantum leap improvements that can happen quickly and reignite results.

The Guiding Principles of the High-Impact Middle Management System

Every management system is built on a set of assumptions and principles. These values form the foundation for each philosophy, technique, and tool included in the system. The High-Impact Middle Management System was designed with eight basic principles in mind. These principles speak to what is unique about middle management and how middle managers produce great results. These guiding principles apply to organizations of any size or in any industry. In addition to providing a theoretical backdrop for the system, the guiding principles of high-impact middle management can be powerful catalytic tools when used as part of a middle manager's definition of success (see chapter 2). Let's look at each principle.

Principle 1: Being a Middle Manager Is Exciting

In almost any company, the most challenging and rewarding jobs will be in middle management. Why? Because middle managers are close to the action, but they also take part in shaping the future strategy and direction of the company. Top executives rarely get to see the action in which middle managers take part, and they also must deal with more bureaucracy and politics. Frontline managers get to see the action but rarely help determine the company's future. As a middle manager, you have your finger on the pulse of the company and can make things happen. Senior executives trust talented middle managers to implement the organization's vision and deliver on its business proposition. And because, in most companies, there are several layers of middle management, most middle managers can enjoy the benefits of this fascinating work while progressing in their career.

Principle 2: Middle Management Is a Craft

The middle manager's job is complex and dynamic, and thus requires focus to deliver results. Weighing competing demands and making choices about how to manage time takes practice and development. As managers grow and mature, they hone their craft and create a style that is effective and unique to them. Along the way, they also learn techniques and practices via mentoring, training, and coaching. The purpose of this book is to help you hone your management skills.

Principle 3: Great Managers Do What Others Don't or Won't

A middle manager's job is littered with tasks that are undesirable, tiring, mundane, or even frightening. Great managers do things that others put off, procrastinate, or ignore. Mediocre managers don't. Not everyone likes to counsel employees or create work plans, but these tasks are necessary and time sensitive.

Principle 4: Beliefs Determine Behavior

Managers act on what they think about most and on what they believe to be true. Their actions come from a set of beliefs formed about job responsibilities, expectations, and reinforcement. To create a different result, you need to adopt a different mindset. Breakthroughs can occur when beliefs line up with efforts to achieve the desired outcome.

Principle 5: Relationships Influence Results

Relationships developed with team members, peers, managers, and customers are important. If you discount relationships, you won't garner the cooperation and support you need from others to produce ideal results— and you are more likely to see your career derail. Great managers develop and maintain positive relationships. Managers who are poor team players or unpleasant to work with are less successful. Many eventually lose their jobs, and most will not progress far. The old admonition rings true here: Never burn your bridges.

Principle 6: Managerial Strengths and Weaknesses Are Known

People notice who is charismatic, who gets defensive, and whether someone is likely to pass the buck. Management is public work, and it is noticed by employees and coworkers every day. Everyone knows who is the best negotiator and who is the underperformer. Because strengths and weaknesses are known, there is no disadvantage to openly discussing them. As a manager, you have a choice to make. You can take an interest in and deal with development needs, or you can ignore them and hope no one notices. But the latter strategy is flawed because people do notice. The only practical and helpful approach is to see faults and failings for what they are and openly discuss them so improvement can occur. Managers should never want to be the last to know if they have a personality trait that is driving people nuts or derailing the work. Those managers who acknowledge the areas where they need to improve will enjoy more support and respect from others than will those who do not.

Principle 7: Great Middle Management Can Be Learned, but One Must "Get It"

Middle management is a craft, a set of practices, and a job that managers can learn with the right training and guidance. Good middle managers are cultivated, not born. Great managers come in wildly different styles and personalities. However, it is essential that all middle managers fully understand their jobs and accountability. Managers who don't take on their role are not likely to succeed and will often see their careers stall or dwindle.

Principle 8: Middle Managers Exist to Make Things Happen

Middle managers are not there to simply oversee what is going to occur on its own. They make a huge difference and play a vital role in improving the business. It is in the face of defeat, during an impending failure, or on the verge of an exciting opportunity that a middle manager's role kicks into high gear. Great middle managers know they exist to make a positive difference and seek out opportunities to make an impact.

Summing Up

These eight guiding principles are reinforced throughout the High-Impact Middle Management System and this book. High-impact middle management is for professional managers who are interested in new or different techniques that will make their work more fruitful and who want to make a difference.

High-Impact Middle Management Generates Results

High-impact middle management builds middle management capacity by developing results-oriented responses (RORs), which are enablers that can have an immediate effect on work. Each high-impact middle management component reinforces and supports the others, so that as you integrate them into your management regimen, the results will improve at a more significant rate than if you had implemented them separately. As you develop your ability to apply RORs in one area, you will also learn skills that will enable you to handle other tasks more effectively. For example, developing dialogue skills for goal setting will also aid you in your ability to use dialogue to improve processes. An ROR is not a technique in itself, but it influences how a technique is used.

Table 1-1 lists several of the RORs used by high-impact middle managers. The results will vary, depending on the choices made about what to do and how to spend time. The RORs are listed on the left side of the table, and low-results responses are listed on the right side. The RORs produce better results. Managers who are dissatisfied with their results can look through this table to discover how to improve their responses.

These RORs can help you focus your time and energy where it will yield the highest benefits (see the 80/20 rule later in this chapter). A quick review of the list of RORs can help get a stalled project or goal moving again. RORs, guiding principles, and a respect for the important and complex nature of the middle manager's job are central to the High-Impact Middle Management System. They come together to help middle managers improve their performance, results, and career success.

How to Apply RORs to Everyday Middle Management Challenges

Steve struggled to understand why the marketing materials produced by his department did not capture the essence of his company's products. He was also frustrated by the fact that while his team members always seemed busy, they were not completing their most important work, such as ensuring the quality of the materials. Was the writing compelling enough? Were the pictures good enough? Did the layout convey the right message? All these

Table 1-1. Results-Oriented Responses Cheat Sheet

Results-oriented responses are listed on the left side of the model and low-results responses on the right side. Responses on the left side produce better results. Managers dissatisfied with their results can look through the model to discover how to improve their responses.

Results-Oriented Responses	Low-Results Responses
Being an owner: Assumes responsibility for the outcome. Takes initiative to make things better. Does whatever it takes to get ideal results. Heart is committed and mind is engaged.	**Being a custodian:** Does only what is required. Waits for others to act. Hopes someone else will take ownership. Avoids that which is unpleasant. Behavior is compliant. Heart and mind not fully engaged.
Being active: Takes the initiative to get things done. Is not easily deterred by setbacks. Proactive. When barriers are present, immediately identifies them and implements an alternative action plan.	**Being passive:** Won't take action unless told to do so. Acts only when necessary. Reactive in stance and style. Barriers and setbacks result in inaction.
Generating: Able to generate new and better alternative approaches and carry them out. Creates from unlimited possibilities. Does not get stuck on how things are already being done.	**Being automatic:** Sticks with the way things have always been done, preserves the status quo. Prefers to act by habit and won't move out of his/her comfort zone. Does not create new approaches or solutions.
Keeping promises: Does what is promised. Fulfills commitments. Keeps his or her word.	**Broken promises or commitments:** Does not follow through with what he or she has promised or committed to. Lets to-do items build up beyond the date expected. Does not follow through on real or implied agreements.
Influencing through enrollment: Influences others by having them see, understand, and take ownership of the goal for themselves. Demonstrates the strategy and plan in such a way that others see and take on the vision for themselves. Others are committed and passionate about the vision and plan.	**Influencing through subtle coercion:** Communicates the vision and plan in a way that resembles a direction or a suggestion. Influences others by making them feel they need to accept and conform. This type of influencing others rarely results in committed and passionate performance.
Being service oriented: Sees his or her role as one that provides service to others. Facilitates cooperation, commitment, and learning. Manages from the mindset, "What can I do to help others excel today?"	**Expecting to be served:** Sees his or her role as one in which people should serve him or her. This stance limits the capacity to have impact on others. Manages from the mindset, "What have you done for me today?"

(continued on next page)

Table 1-1. Results-Oriented Responses Cheat Sheet (continued)	

Results-Oriented Responses	Low-Results Responses
Being coachable: Accepts and uses feedback, input, criticism, and ideas from others and is curiously observant. Is not defensive when given feedback. Recognizes that others have something to offer.	**Being uncoachable:** Blocks the environment from being influential, puts up barriers. Focuses more on being right, looking good, and appearing in charge.
Practicing quality dialogue: Communicates with the intent of making a difference or moving a topic forward. Engages in active conversation focused on the topic at hand.	**Using dialogue without purpose:** Communicates in a way that does not move the topic forward. Spends time discussing rumors, gossip, complaints, diversions, whining, and opinions not helpful toward enabling the desired result.

Source: Adapted from *H.I.M.M. (High Impact Middle Management): Solutions for Today's Busy Managers,* by Lisa Haneberg. More information is available in chapter 1, or visit www.lisahaneberg.com.

areas were part of the problem, but the underlying cause of the quality problem was less specific. How was Steve approaching the problem? Were his responses likely to lead to success or failure? Reviewing just a few items on the list of RORs sheds some light on his situation:

- Being an owner—Steve owned his role as functional leader, but he also let the fact that he had inherited the process slow down his efforts to improve it. There was an opportunity for him to improve results by taking more ownership of how he wanted the department to run currently, rather than going with the status quo.

- Being active—Steve had implemented a few small ideas and new actions. However, he would be able to realize more significant improvements if he would take action in a more meaningful way.

- Generating—Steve was a very creative manager, so generating new ideas would not have been a problem—if it hadn't been for the issue of people. He was allowing his preconceptions of what the current team players would accept or reject to curtail his natural tendency to be a creative problem solver.

By looking at just three RORs, Steve could create several potential approaches for how to improve the production process. High-impact middle management uses the elegant simplicity of the RORs as a basis for each specific technique. As you review each suggestion, you can return to the list of RORs in table 1-1 and see how it ties into at least one preferred response.

The 80/20 Rule

In the early 1900s, the economist Vilfredo Pareto established the Pareto Principle, otherwise known as the 80/20 rule. He found that 20 percent of the population owned 80 percent of the land in Italy. He then noticed that this ratio applied to other things in science, business, and life. The 80/20 rule asserts that in any given situation, 20 percent of the work performed will account for 80 percent of the results. Conversely, the other 80 percent of the work will yield only 20 percent of the results. Thus, a few actions will make a greater proportional impact. The 80/20 rule is also used to evaluate errors and problems; therefore, the top 20 percent of systemic problems causes 80 percent of the inefficiencies.

The High-Impact Middle Management System applies the 80/20 rule to many aspects of middle management. Thus, just a few methods practiced together will have a significant impact on results and execution. High-impact middle management focuses on the 20 percent of the effort that will yield 80 percent of the impact for busy middle managers, and it highlights the 20 percent of actions that matter most.

The High-Impact Middle Management System was built on the premise that a middle manager's job is challenging, complex, and very important to a corporation's success. As a middle manager, you have the opportunity to do work that is meaningful and exciting. The right training and development can help frustrated or unsuccessful middle managers become high-impact middle managers. Unfortunately, most middle managers are so busy and overwhelmed that they are not likely to take the time to attend training classes. That is a shame, because mastering middle management is much easier with good coaching and guidance. The High-Impact Middle Management System presented in this book will teach time-pressed middle managers what they can do differently that will offer the greatest benefit to their team and their organization.

Chapter 2

How to Think Like a High-Impact Middle Manager

How a middle manager approaches a situation can either help or hinder the results he or she is seeking. Thoughts and beliefs can limit opportunities or, conversely, enable options to be discovered and considered. High-impact middle managers select beliefs that support their goals. When your thinking is aligned with the larger objective, productive actions naturally happen and lead to positive results.

Success Stories

Many well-known business success stories illustrate the power of aligning beliefs with company goals. A belief may seem like a tiny inconsequential thing, but it can get an organization rolling in the right direction. The reverse is also true. Stagnant thinking that is not aligned with goals can contribute to the downfall of a company or department. Let's look at a few examples of successful leaders who recognized the importance of beliefs and how those beliefs make an impact on business results.

More Than Sausage

"If it is to be, it is up to me. If it is up to me, it shall be." Thousands of managers have heard Ralph Stayer, the CEO of Johnsonville Sausage, say these words during talks at corporations around the world. Johnson-ville Sausage has enjoyed significant and lasting success with Stayer at the helm. The company is famous for its bottom-up, top-down integration of ownership and innovation that creates the best and most popular sausage products on the market today.

In his best-selling business book *Flight of the Buffalo: Soaring to Excellence, Learning to Let Employees Lead*, Stayer describes the importance of productive thoughts and the breakthroughs he experienced by aligning his beliefs for success: "I learned to change from being a victim to being responsible by asking myself, 'What am I doing or not doing that causes the situation I don't like?' Restating the problem into factors that I control helps me feel, and be, powerful." Part of Stayer's leadership mantra is to first assume that "I am the problem" and then approach each improvement opportunity from there.

Direct to You

In his book *Direct from Dell*, Michael Dell wrote:

> Our success is due, in part, to not just an ability, but a willingness, to look at things differently. I believe opportunity is part instinct and part immersion—in an industry, a subject, or an area of expertise. Dell is proof that people can learn to recognize and take advantage of opportunities that others are convinced don't exist. You don't have to be a genius, or a visionary, or even a college graduate to think unconventionally. You just need a framework and a dream.

Michael Dell started his computer company in 1984 with $1,000 and a dream to one day be as big as IBM. By 1998, the Dell Computer Corporation was taking in $12 million in sales over the Internet each day; and by 2003, it was number 36 on the *Fortune* 500 list. The Dell business model changed the way all computer manufacturers do business, including how they go to market, manage inventory, and produce products.

Delivery You Can Count On

"Back in 1971, my belief was that you could run these small, high-value-added computer parts through this hub-and-spokes system. Also, I did something else a little bit unusual, which was to combine the airplanes and trucks into one delivery system. This didn't seem to me to be so controversial, but all the traditional people felt that it was highly iconoclastic. So that's the genesis of Federal Express." This is how Fred Smith, CEO of FedEx, described the thinking behind this successful business launch in 1971 in a recent *Fortune* magazine article.

Over the last three decades, FedEx has revolutionized the shipping business. Smith believed the shipping business could work in the same way banks clear checks: through a hub-and-spokes system. By applying this model to shipping, FedEx delivered on a promise of service consistency, speed, and accuracy. Since the launch of FedEx, UPS and the U.S. Postal Service have come out with similar services to match the breadth of shipping choices, reliability, and efficiency that FedEx has achieved.

Turning Beliefs into Results

Each of these stories illustrates how powerful, positive, and focused beliefs lead to favorable results and how thoughts affect actions. By adopting beliefs that served their goals, Stayer, Dell, and Smith produced outstanding results. Successes, a few setbacks, and a drive to continue the move forward characterized their journeys. Some of their beliefs have remained the same, while others have changed as needed to serve their goals. These CEOs know that how they approach running their businesses has contributed to their successes.

When results are lacking, the first thing to look at is the underlying beliefs that are driving actions. The relationship between beliefs and actions is important. Actions come from beliefs, and actions and results reinforce beliefs. This cycle can help or hinder success. Figure 2-1 shows how beliefs get in the way of results. Notice how the cycle reinforces the status quo and increases the manager's levels of stress and frustration.

Figure 2-2 depicts a more productive belief-action cycle. This model shows how helpful beliefs lead to productive actions and improved results. These results reinforce proactive and positive beliefs. The difference between those beliefs that serve a manager's goals and those that do not is easy to distinguish when both are examined closely.

Figure 2-1. A Typical Belief-Action Cycle

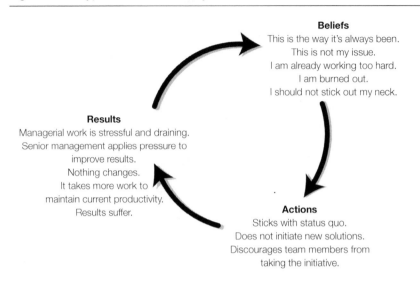

Beliefs
This is the way it's always been.
This is not my issue.
I am already working too hard.
I am burned out.
I should not stick out my neck.

Results
Managerial work is stressful and draining.
Senior management applies pressure to
improve results.
Nothing changes.
It takes more work to
maintain current productivity.
Results suffer.

Actions
Sticks with status quo.
Does not initiate new solutions.
Discourages team members from
taking the initiative.

Figure 2-2. The High-Impact Middle Management Belief-Action Cycle

Beliefs
I need to fix this.
We will save time and effort
in the long run.
Something must change to produce
different results.
This is why I am here.

Results
Problems get resolved.
Opportunities are recognized and seized.
The business improves.
Failures are quickly reworked.
Managerial work is fruitful
and meaningful.

Actions
Initiates improvements.
Open to new ideas.
Team members encouraged
to think.
Team members encouraged
to offer ideas.

High-impact middle managers get better results by taking on a set of beliefs—called a definition of success—that will be most useful and by abandoning those beliefs or mindsets that will not serve them well. All managers have a definition of success, and it is important to know whether your definition of success is helping you, and your team, get where you want to go or getting in the way. High-impact middle managers have a definition of success that leads to ideal results and personal satisfaction.

Examining Your Beliefs

People spend most of their waking hours in conversation—not with others, but with themselves. The mind, on both the conscious and unconscious levels, is constantly processing internal chatter or "self-talk." The internal dialogue that is most critical for managers is that regarding the beliefs they hold about accomplishment and failure.

These messages are particularly powerful because they shape the choices you make and how you look at your job. Imagine what would happen if you believed that being strong meant winning arguments at any cost. You would probably act like an obnoxious control freak and alienate others. This would not yield good results. If another middle manager adopted the belief that disagreements should be handled in a manner that preserves and strengthens relationships, he or she would approach things differently, and the results would be more productive. When managers examine and realign their definition of success, they can experience improved results and perhaps an immediate breakthrough.

What Is Your Definition of Success?

Your definition of success is the collection of beliefs you hold that affects how you choose to manage. These beliefs determine how you will approach making decisions, including which activities you will tend to favor and which you might avoid. They also influence how you react during times of stress, failure, success, and creativity. They include

- beliefs about how success is achieved
- beliefs about what success looks like

- beliefs about what is expected
- beliefs reinforced by past successes and failures
- comparative assumptions about what has made others successful
- beliefs, whether positive or negative, passed on by your role models
- beliefs not readily admitted or recognized until examined in detail
- beliefs that can be changed instantaneously.

As a middle manager, you should regularly evaluate and realign your definition of success. Though this may seem straightforward, the process can be tricky because some beliefs are unknown or not recognized. It is common, for example, to verbally define success as one thing and then behave in a contrary way. Verbally, a manager might say that success means achieving results for the benefit of the company and its employees, while behaviorally he or she indicates that success means being right and in control.

To develop the capacity to recognize the beliefs that make up your definition of success, write down five recent actions and ask "What beliefs led to these actions?" Be wary of your natural inclination to define logical reasoning as the belief that led to your actions. There are many potential beliefs behind an action, so it is best to identify the possibilities and then select the correct motive—for examples, see exercise 2-1.

People who are always late to meetings may not consciously think "My time is more important," but there is a belief that is making being late an acceptable action. To change the behavior, a new belief needs to take its place, such as "I am expected to be on time" or "being on time shows respect for my peers."

High-Impact Middle Management Thinking about Success

How do high-impact middle managers define success? Each middle manager is going to hold beliefs specific to his or her function and current goals, because those elements are unique. Many aspects of middle management, however, are similar across industries. When observing and talking with high-impact middle managers, it becomes apparent that they

Exercise 2-1. Behaviors and Potential Beliefs

Behavior	Potential Beliefs
Always comes to meetings on time	• Professionals show up to meetings on time. • It is important to respect the time of others. • I am expected to be on time. • If I am late, I will miss something.
Always late to meetings	• Everyone is always late. • It is not important to be on time. • My timetable is more important. • I will not miss anything; this is not worthwhile. • Nobody cares if I am late. • I am too busy to be on time.
Defensive when being given feedback	• I need to prove that I am right. • People who are weak need input and help. • I look bad when others challenge my ideas. • I need to win to feel good. • I do not value the other person's input. • I am embarrassed when challenged in public.
Micromanages	• I am expected to stay on top of the details. • If I do not check up on them, they will not complete the work to my satisfaction. • My employees cannot be trusted. • My employees constantly need my help. • This is what good management looks like. • I would rather work with my employees doing these tasks than spend time doing other tasks.

(continued on next page)

Exercise 2-1. Behaviors and Potential Beliefs (continued)

Behavior	Potential Beliefs
Does not share input in meetings when the agenda is known ahead of time	• I prefer to think things through before commenting. • If he wants my opinion, he will ask me. • I do not want to stick my neck out by sharing my ideas. • This is not my meeting; I am not the leader. • I am not expected to contribute in this meeting.
Regularly discusses ideas and issues with manager	• I am expected to form and share ideas and issues. • My manager wants to hear from me. • I need to make sure my manager knows about the key issues within my area. • Managers should toot their own horn to get noticed.
Communicates with manager only when asked and only on topics asked about	• When it comes to my manager, no news is good news. • Managing on my own is a sign of strength; if I ask my manager to review what's going on, this shows that I am weak and need his help. • My manager is too busy to talk to me; I am not a priority.
Avoids coaching others	• If I talk to her, it will make things worse between us. • The discomfort of the conversation will outweigh any benefits. • She will come around on her own. • I have too many tasks to do that are more important. • I don't want to do this.
Does not hesitate to tackle tough personnel issues or to deal with poor performers	• It is my responsibility to handle this issue—it cannot wait. • Performance can only improve if it is dealt with. • If I say nothing, she will more likely fail in the end. • I am accountable for ensuring that everyone performs; there can be no "deadweight" on the team.

share similar beliefs about what success means and how it can best be achieved. What's more, these same beliefs are often held by successful senior executives. This is important to note, because a senior manager's expectations of his or her middle managers will tend to reflect his or her own beliefs about how success is achieved. An additional benefit of high-impact middle management thinking is that it will serve middle managers well throughout their career progression. High-impact middle managers subscribe to these beliefs:

- Middle managers are expected to be accountable and take ownership; high-impact middle management is built on the philosophy that to achieve results, middle managers need to take ownership of whatever needs to be done. This belief drives proactivity and helps to stave off procrastination.
- Middle managers are expected to make a positive contribution to the business; a middle manager's job is to think creatively and proactively, and take initiative to improve his or her performance and his or her team's performance. This belief reinforces the concept that it is not a middle manager's job to maintain or oversee what would otherwise happen on its own.
- Middle managers should be outstanding role models because they influence the culture and tone of the business; it is not OK for middle managers to be unprofessional or model undesirable behaviors. You will enjoy more success as a manager if you take your role as a professional seriously and recognize that your team members and peers are watching and emulating you when they decide how they should respond to situations.
- Middle managers need to get results; middle managers who believe that it is their job to execute work and deliver results are more likely to choose results-oriented responses and actions. They are also more apt to value productivity measurements and process improvements as tools to monitor, manage, and enhance results.
- Management is a social as well as a business function; with every meeting you attend and every conversation in which you participate, there is an opportunity to either add to or detract from the

quality of the relationship(s). Middle managers need the support and cooperation of those with whom they work. Operating in isolation will not yield success. Recognizing this fact will help you choose responses that preserve and build relationships rather than those that destroy communication.

- Flexible and nimble teams are more successful; middle managers must have their finger on the pulse of the company and know when changes in approach make sense and would be of benefit. A manager who holds this belief is more open to exploring options and creative solutions and is less likely to become comfortable with the status quo.

- Being a middle manager is to play a key role; middle managers should want to spend most of their time managing and facilitating the work of others. Middle managers who do not believe their job is interesting and desirable will not likely serve themselves, or their organization, well.

- Success means delivering results and managing people to achieve optimal productivity and satisfaction; to be truly effective as a high-impact middle manager, you must reframe your definition of success. Success should be defined more by accomplishments and less by promotions, status, or other extrinsically motivating factors such as cash bonuses.

- Good managers are responsive to the ideas and concerns of others; being defensive or combative does not reflect favorably on any manager. Being open and flexible makes one seem more intelligent and talented. If you have the constant need to prove that you are right, you will undermine relationships with your superiors and your subordinates.

This list of beliefs forms a powerful definition of success! However, you will naturally adopt beliefs specific to challenges you are facing. For example, if over the next year the focus needs to be on product development, you will adopt beliefs and create a vision about how to best manage product development and what outstanding product development looks like.

Imagine what a workplace would look and feel like if all middle managers took on this definition of success. The atmosphere would be electric, exciting, and highly productive. What a great place to work! Here's the amazing part: You can adopt these beliefs right now and they will begin to work immediately. To make the high-impact middle management definition of success a part of your daily management regimen, you should review the beliefs listed on the previous pages and create a list of supporting actions you can take today. Do this daily until the practice has become second nature. The Results-Oriented Responses Cheat Sheet (see table 1-1 and chapter 14) and High-Impact Middle Management Scorecard (see figure 14-1) will also help you incorporate this definition of success into your daily regimen. Incorporating these beliefs into your daily and weekly planning will help foster responses that will improve results. For some middle managers, the changes may be so striking that they experience a breakthrough.

Discard Definitions of Success That Produce Failure

In addition to adopting new beliefs that support goals, you may need to discard old beliefs that are not useful or are not serving you well. How do you know if your definition of success is constructive? These questions can help you diagnose whether your current beliefs are helpful or harmful:

1. Are results coming in as expected? If not, why not? What beliefs might be responsible for this shortfall?
2. On average, how much time do you spend being reactive versus being proactive? If you spend more time being reactive, why? What beliefs support a focus on reactivity?
3. Have tasks been pushed aside, delayed, or ignored? If yes, why? What's driving this procrastination?
4. Does feedback or criticism result in a defensive comeback, shutdown of communication, or combative posture? Why is it important to you to be right or to win?
5. Who in the organization is your most positive and powerful role model? What does he or she do that is so effective? Which beliefs would support these behaviors?

6. Are team members satisfied with their jobs? Are they frustrated or burned out? If so, why is this the case, and what is the manager's role in fixing this?

7. How enjoyable is middle management? If it is not satisfying work, why not? Are there new beliefs that you could adopt to improve your job satisfaction and your impact on the company?

On the basis of your answers to these questions, you can begin to recognize unhelpful beliefs and redesign your definition of success. Your nonproductive beliefs also become apparent when you examine disappointments as they occur. For example, if a project did not go well, do a postmortem to discover why this was the case and to understand the thinking that allowed the failure to occur. Was it a lack of follow-up? Too little research before implementation? Whatever the reasons, the actions that were taken came from supporting beliefs. Did you assume that everyone would do his or her work on time and that follow-up should not be required? Did you believe that the key vendor had done the research and that nothing would likely go wrong? What if you had taken on the belief that frequent follow-up meetings would be helpful in keeping everyone on track and uncovering areas where the project could get derailed? Would the results have been any different? Yes, they certainly would have.

Besides the definition of success presented above, you, as a middle manager, can define the beliefs that will best serve your goals by completing this exercise:

1. Create a list of management goals for the coming year. These goals should spell out important accomplishments, key initiatives, and areas that will need special managerial attention.

2. For each goal, identify beliefs that would support success. In other words, what mindset is going to best facilitate goal attainment?

As Ralph Stayer wrote in *Flight of the Buffalo*, "I understand that I am the problem. Accepting that enables me to be the solution." Middle managers who align their beliefs to support their goals will enjoy more success and greater accomplishment. The high-impact middle management definition of success provides middle managers with a way of thinking about their jobs that is invigorating and dynamic, and that delivers results. This, coupled with beliefs that support specific goals, establishes a winning foundation for any middle manager's journey toward success.

High-impact middle managers pay attention to how well their definition of success is serving them. They know that there is a strong link among beliefs, actions, and results. These successful managers have learned that to improve results, beliefs that are more effective may need to be adopted while other less effective beliefs need to be discarded. High-impact middle management thinking is a distillation of powerful beliefs that can help busy middle managers excel and enjoy their work.

Chapter 3

Power Partnerships

Clark was a successful and influential vice president of human resources (HR). His peers and other senior managers valued his input
and participation. They involved Clark and his department managers in
the day-to-day operations of their respective departments. Clark's HR
department was effective and well respected to a degree rarely found in
most companies. Because of the fantastic partnership between Clark's
staff and other departments within the organization, Clark and his team
made a positive impact on the company. However, it wasn't just a one-
way street—other departments influenced Clark and his team as well.

Clark was thus a powerful role model who demonstrated how internal departments should collaborate to service one another and achieve
results. Clark also reinforced this belief in collaboration when it came
time to promote and evaluate his team members. Other divisions regularly sought out candidates from his department, and he frequently
championed his staff for internal promotions and other positions within
the company.

What made Clark's collaborative approach even more impressive
was the fact that his company had a very competitive environment.
Department leaders were more inclined to exclude, rather than include,
members of internal service teams, like HR. Had it not been for the foundation of partnership that Clark had established, other vice presidents

in the company would not have given the HR department the same level of consideration or included its staff in as many initiatives.

Lonny could have learned a few things from Clark. Lonny thought the best way to get ahead was to flatter and try to impress senior management. He took credit for work performed by others on his team to make it appear that he was the one who had dreamed up the idea. In meetings, he was a yes man, always agreeing with higher-level managers to get their nod of approval. He applied for two promotions, for which he was technically qualified, but he was turned down for both of them. The fact was that other managers did not feel they could trust him or that he shared their goals. They feared that his personal drive for self-promotion would overshadow the needs of his team and those of the company.

Teamwork Drives Accomplishment

Everyone wants recognition and validation. Evening news programs love to feature stories of heroes who save the day. In the business world, however, the best and most effective way to achieve results is through teamwork—especially at the middle management level. A group of talented people rallying behind a single cause creates more success than a lone individual going off on his or her own. Middle managers who are good at collaborating are significantly more successful than those who try to go it alone. Clark understood this and was successful. Lonny did not and suffered the consequences professionally.

Developing and maintaining productive partnerships is an important skill for any manager—but most particularly for the high-impact middle manager. Why? Because unlike senior executives, who give directives, middle managers more often than not do not have unilateral decision-making authority. Effective partnerships are a middle manager's currency for getting the work done.

In most companies, departments are interdependent. When things go well, it is rarely because of a single department. It takes many teams, firing on all cylinders, to produce the best results. Middle managers can facilitate their teams' success by working together. By collaborating to improve the performance levels of other teams, middle managers can improve the productivity of their own area.

Middle managers need the cooperation and support of their peers when opportunity knocks or problems occur. Middle managers who take the time to gain peer support for new ideas and initiatives will find that implementation is easier and more trouble free. Effective high-impact middle managers know that their peers are a rich source of ideas and new approaches.

Partners also warn each other about emerging problems and lend a hand to avert a crisis. Communication happens on many levels in most organizations. Some topics are reviewed and discussed in staff meetings. Other information gets sent to employees via email. Sanitized and spun messages are presented to the public. Then there is the dialogue that occurs during informal conversations and lunchtime chats. This last type of information, the informal and unwritten communication, is very important. Emerging concerns, pending decisions, potentially troublesome rumors, and fresh new ideas are most likely to be heard in these outlets first.

To ensure they are part of this communication pipeline, middle managers need to develop and maintain excellent relationships with their peers and managers. Working well with other managers also makes their work more meaningful and satisfying. When the members of a management team work together, the pace of work quickens and the energy is more positive and oriented toward success. Even when faced with significant challenges, a strong and collaborative management team can make the challenge about finding a creative solution and not about the "problem."

The Traits of Partnership

Effective partnership helps organizations deal with tough challenges and times of growth and opportunity. Every organization and department can benefit from the coordinated efforts of their talented managers. Partnership goes beyond cooperation to become a purposeful act of inclusion, collaboration, and comanagement. Merely being helpful when solicited or asked does not make one an effective partner. Partners seek each other out and proactively involve each other in day-to-day management conversations and decisions. Effective partnership emerges from a combination of several traits:

- shared purpose
- shared ownership
- mutual trust
- critical thinking
- shared success and failure
- effective inclusion and communication.

Let's look at each one.

Shared Purpose

Partners, by definition, are linked to one another. In the business world, partners need to have a sense that they are striving for the same goal. When middle managers have a shared goal, their work together has purpose and meaning. A common target provides a foundation for partnership. Their opinions and perspectives may differ significantly, but if they are all reaching for the same goal, they can find common ground. To create a shared purpose, spend time with other middle managers learning about and discussing one another's goals and challenges.

Shared Ownership

When two or more managers share ownership of a result or outcome, they are more likely to work together effectively. Co-owning an outcome takes partnership a step beyond cooperation to collaboration. Senior managers who instill a sense of shared ownership among their middle managers will find that this expectation helps drive middle managers to partner with peers, other departments, and clients more often and more effectively. You should have periodic conversations with your peers to clarify roles and expectations in areas of shared ownership. Maintaining an open and positive dialogue will help both of you ensure that your respective areas are optimally managed to produce results.

Mutual Trust

Middle managers who trust one another will partner together more effectively. Mutual trust facilitates openness, creativity, and communication. Managers do not need to agree or see things identically to develop trusting and respectful relationships with one another. Often, an appreciation of diverse thoughts and ideas improves the regard managers have for one another. Middle managers who collaborate well almost always share mutual trust for one another. This trust is built through the process of active and healthy collaboration and comanagement. By practicing the high-impact power partnership techniques that are given in the next section, middle managers can begin to build a history together that will enhance trust and openness.

Critical Thinking

Without critical thinking, partnership is just small talk. The essence of collaboration is the act of solving problems and generating new ideas together. This work occurs best when all parties are mentally stimulated, productive, and encouraged to think critically. Results are built on the mental capabilities of middle managers working together. High-impact middle managers engage their peers in provocative and useful dialogue. They ask open-ended questions and seek ideas for addressing business problems.

Shared Success and Failure

Middle managers build stronger partnerships when they share the experience of winning and losing. There is nothing like seeing a project through to completion as a team. If the project is a success, celebrating together reinforces the positive aspects of collaboration. When failures occur, middle managers should huddle together to turn the loss into a win. Sharing successes and failures brings the cycle of partnership full circle.

Effective Inclusion and Communication

Partners talk with each other often and take the initiative to include each other in formative planning and brainstorming conversations. Just as the middle manager should feel a sense of responsibility about communicating effectively with his or her employees, he or she should also expect to keep fellow middle managers in the loop.

Summing Up

The traits of partnership outlined above describe what peer-to-peer collaboration looks like in action. How do you know if you have been a good partner? You can ask a trusted friend or colleague, although the answer will generally be more favorable than objective. You can also ask your manager. But, again, managers may find it difficult to share their concerns and criticisms openly. A better strategy is to read organizational clues. Middle managers should observe how other managers interact with one another and compare this with their own experience. Middle managers can also gauge the type of partner they have been by looking at informal communication practices. How often do your peers stop by and ask for input? How open and lively are your conversations with colleagues? Look for examples of successes and failures that illustrate good or poor partnership practices. By asking questions of your peers, managers, and coworkers and then watching how they respond and interact, you can begin to glean insight into the type of partner you have been.

High-Impact Middle Management Power Partnership Techniques

High-impact middle managers have learned what it takes to be a great partner. They know that the benefits of effective collaboration far outweigh the time and effort expended in creating the partnership. High-impact middle managers also know that good partnerships do not simply happen. There are eight techniques that they must practice and cultivate to increase the benefits of peer-to-peer collaboration. Let's look at each one.

Technique 1: Resist the Need to Control

If you have a constant need to control situations, people, or conversations, it will undermine effective collaboration with your peer group. Partnering is a give-and-take process in which no one gets to play boss.

Listen and watch for both verbal and nonverbal clues that suggest other people are feeling pressured or pushed. One of the best ways to give up control in a conversation is to ask more open-ended questions and make fewer opinionated statements.

Technique 2: Spend Time with Peers

Management is a social act. The more time that middle managers spend working with one another, the easier and more natural the partnering process will feel. In addition, peers that get together often feel more comfortable asking for input, help, and participation than do those who avoid each other. Middle managers who engage peers only when necessary will receive a cooler and less helpful response. Great middle managers, both extroverts and introverts, know the value of cultivating and building relationships.

Technique 3: Resolve Any Past Partnership Failures

Old conflicts and arguments affect how people relate to one another in the present and future. You need to take the initiative to resolve any prior relationship issues so as to pave the way for better and more productive collaboration in the future. The benefits of working through and getting past prior problems with other managers will more than make up for the initial discomfort of broaching the topic with them. Managers who resolve their differences will also feel less work-related stress.

If you are faced with a peer who does not seem willing to improve the relationship, you can do one of three things. First, you might try a different approach. Can you look at the situation from his or her perspective? Have you isolated the key issues or problems? It may be that what you thought was the problem is not what is actually bothering this person. Second, you are the only person you can control. Even if your peer is hanging onto a grudge, make sure that you continue to act and relate in a manner that is professional and collaborative. If you continue to take the high road, he or she might come around in time. Your third option, and the most dramatic, is to work with other peers whenever possible. You may still need to conduct business with this person, but when given the choice, it is most productive to work with those who reciprocate.

Technique 4: Communicate on Behalf of Your Peers

Effective communication is one of the most reliable predictors of a healthy partnership. Managers who keep one another in the loop and represent one another well in meetings and other conversations are generally great partners. Communicating with peers should be a regular part of your day. In addition to communicating well with one another, it is important for peers to communicate well on one another's behalf.

High-impact middle managers are willing and able to represent their peer's interests and needs when that person is not present in staff meetings, brainstorming sessions, and informal conversations. You may need to defend a peer's budget choices, or remind others of his or her projects that will require resources, or, more commonly, represent his or her opinions and concerns. Great partners do this even when they do not agree with their peer's point of view. When representing your middle manager peers in a positive light, you communicate that respect and care for colleagues is a key organizational value.

Technique 5: If You Cannot Say Anything Nice, Do Not Say Anything at All

Never bad-mouth peers in front of others. It never pays to talk badly about peers, and it will burn bridges that you will need later on. Speak respectfully about other managers, even if you think ill of them. Managers who talk about other people behind their backs end up looking bad themselves. It is immature, unprofessional, and destructive to bad-mouth peers. The saying "What goes around, comes around" certainly applies to workplace relationships. This is not to say that disagreements with peers should be ignored. The best way to deal with a difference of opinion or disagreement is to communicate it directly, in a productive way, to the person involved.

Technique 6: Take Ownership of Problems and Challenges

Don't pass the buck. Few situations can put a damper on a partnership faster than being hung out to dry by a peer. Catherine learned this the hard way. Harry blamed her for problems that were rooted in his organization. When the president confronted Catherine about this, she was unfairly put on the defensive. Harry's choice to pass blame and abdicate his own involvement in the problem diminished the level of partnership that he and Catherine would have in the future.

High-impact middle managers own problems and concerns and do not shift the blame onto other managers. If you have a complaint about how another manager is handling a situation, speak with that manager directly before taking it to the next level of management or that individual's boss. If not, you could burn bridges not only with your peer but with upper management as well. If you do need to communicate an issue to another manager, then present a fair and balanced view of the problem, including the part of it that you own.

Technique 7: Graciously Share Credit

Partners know that successes come from collaboration and that all players should share the credit. Though it may be true that one person's idea was the catalyst for the breakthrough, the overall success was a product of the joint effort. Middle managers who ensure that everyone feels a part of the success will enjoy a positive momentum going into the next project or initiative.

Technique 8: Know the Needs and Concerns of Peers, Managers, Customers, and Employees

Middle managers will find it is easier to be good partners when they understand the needs and motivations of those with whom they regularly work. They will be in a position to anticipate needs, warn of emerging problems, and share ideas with peers if they know what is important to others. As a middle manager, you should be able to answer these questions about your employees and the other managers with whom you work on a daily basis:

- What are their needs? What are their goals? What is their purpose in the organization?
- What are their interests? What are their motivations? (These are often different from their needs.)
- What are their strengths and weaknesses? What unique skills and talents do they bring to the organization?

- What are their hot buttons? What frustrates them most?
- How do they react to changes?
- What do I expect from them? What do they expect from me and my department?

Case Study

John and Barry were vice presidents reporting to the division president. They were both very talented and opinionated. When they were together in meetings, their demeanor toward one another was either cool and aloof or confrontational. The real problem, however, came when they were not together. Both John and Barry took cheap shots at each other's expense in front of others. They also did not involve each other in decisions as often as they should have, preferring to avoid one another when possible. Barry was particularly critical and cynical of John and many of his group members. Neither was an inexperienced middle manager; they should have known better than to relate in this dysfunctional way. However, even managers with decades of experience let their opinions and emotions get the best of them.

As if the poor relations between John and Barry were not enough, the managers who reported to John and Barry were beginning to emulate the dysfunction between them. It took having a manager who worked for John and worked closely with Barry to call their attention to what was going on. To their credit, once they saw the impact their poor relationship was having on their results and their teams, they were able to become effective partners. In just a couple months, the improvement was significant, and both were realizing benefits in terms of productivity and worker satisfaction.

Summing Up

Middle managers who practice the eight partnering techniques outlined above will see immediate and long-term benefits. When peers become advocates and coaches, they add value to each other's quests for results and efficiency. Being a good partner will also reflect well on you and improve your ability to be promoted and valued within the organization.

Effective partnerships are valuable assets for managers. Developing and maintaining productive relationships with peers, managers, and team members allows high-impact middle managers to extend their reach into the organization and improve their effectiveness. Great partners share ownership for projects, and they work together collectively to enjoy success and recover from failure. Power partnership techniques—such as spending more time with peers, resolving relationship issues, and representing others well—can help middle managers improve peer relationships.

Planning for Execution

The Reality Check: Measuring Current Performance

Until his last day of work, Tom would have said that his performance was meeting the expectations of his manager. Unfortunately, he was dead wrong. Tom was a poor manager, and his boss felt that Tom and his team did not produce satisfactory work. Tom was not an effective communicator, and others felt he was untrustworthy. His manager had asked for changes that he neither implemented nor delegated to his team—even though he had told his manager he would. Several conversations occurred between Tom and his manager, but Tom was never able to grasp where things stood or how his manager viewed his performance.

When people in the home office spoke about Tom's colleague, Ron, their eyes would roll and they would exchange a familiar look of, "Oh, that guy." Senior managers felt that Ron was a marginal manager, someone they would replace if they could find a better alternative. Unfortunately, he had specialized technical skills that made him hard to replace. Ron openly disparaged the company, as well as its policies and procedures. He seemed to take pride in being disrespectful and insubordinate in front of his employees. In addition, his lack of professionalism and negative demeanor rubbed off on others. A highly respected manager became a marginally performing employee after working only a few short months under Ron's supervision. Turnover on Ron's team was high. What was perhaps most unbelievable was the fact that even though he was open and brash with his opinions and criticisms, Ron had no idea that the senior management team held him in such low regard.

Jane, however, preferred to see the bright side of every story. Her glass was always half full. Though this perspective served her well in many situations, when it came to her job, her Pollyanna take on things became her undoing. She managed a department that produced several major projects each year, but she could not get the work done on time or in an organized fashion. Her manager had several specific conversations with her about areas where she needed to improve, but she did not internalize the feedback and correct her performance. She chose, instead, to believe that as long as she worked hard, everything would be fine. "I'm doing the best I can," became a frequent response when her manager asked questions about late projects. She was in denial.

Unlike Tom, Ron, or Jane, Bob was smart, creative, and a great asset to the company. Yet he had no idea that several senior managers thought he was one of the more important managers on the team. He knew that he was doing OK but did not feel the level of satisfaction and acknowledgment equal to his managers' opinion of his performance. When times were tough and the organization needed to reduce staff, he worried that he would be first on the list of expendable managers. In reality, he was on the list of managers who were too important to let go.

Tom, Ron, Jane, and Bob all suffered from a poor or inaccurate definition of how their managers and the organization viewed their performance. Unfortunately, this is a common problem that gets in the way of a middle manager's ability to be successful. The reason this was the case may be obvious with Tom, Ron, and Jane, because their performance was unsatisfactory and their careers were in jeopardy. But Bob's inaccurate perception about his performance also affected his success, even though he underestimated his value and worth to the organization.

When you, as a middle manager, are unaware of or unclear about your current performance levels, it is difficult for you to set appropriate goals and targets. Efforts to improve need to begin with a benchmark and need to include a plan for transitioning from today's reality to tomorrow's goal. You can best improve results when you understand

- how your manager would evaluate your performance
- your reputation among managers, employees, and peers
- how well your teams are meeting goals and producing results
- how others would describe your teams' contributions and effectiveness.

Most middle managers do not have an understanding of all these areas because open, candid, and helpful feedback is not the norm in most organizations. This is a shame, because knowledge about current performance is instrumental to most plans for change and improvement. Many efforts at change fail because they do not consider and incorporate today's realities. Ignorance is definitely not bliss when it comes to managing people, projects, and processes.

For middle managers to produce the best results possible, when making all goals and plans, they need to recognize and consider current levels of performance. It is critical that you know how your superiors, peers, and employees view your performance. If you have established the right benchmark, or starting point, improvement plans will be more realistic and operational.

The reality check is a set of techniques that you can use to understand your own performance level and the current effectiveness of your team. These techniques include methods for

- assessing your reputation within the organization
- assessing your team's reputation within the organization
- measuring your team's performance against goals and results
- communicating current performance findings to your managers and team members.

High-impact middle managers have a strong self-awareness and know how to keep their ears to the ground to listen for valuable information about how they and their teams are doing. The journey from good to great, or great to greater, is paved with well-planned initiatives and improvement efforts. High-impact middle managers have learned that successfully planned and implemented improvement initiatives start with good information.

How to Assess Your Reputation within the Organization

Middle managers must understand the reputation they have in their organization, whether it is positive or not as good as they would like. Peers, managers, and team members respond differently to each middle manager based on past results and how that manager has reacted in good times and bad. The quality of his or her relationships plays a big part in determining a manager's reputation. Middle managers with poor reputations will find it harder to garner support for initiatives and will likely not receive full and helpful collaborative efforts from others.

When people say that a manager has a good reputation, they are saying that he or she

- Can be trusted—managers are perceived as trustworthy when their words and actions are consistent. Trustworthiness is also affected by a middle manager's ability to keep confidences and represent others in a positive and professional way. Being caught talking about someone behind his or her back is a quick way to become known as untrustworthy.
- Does what he or she promises—keeping promises means doing what was agreed to, whether the agreement was spoken, written, or implied. Fulfilling implied agreements is just as important as keeping promises etched in stone or email. Middle managers who follow through on the commitments they make have integrity and will enjoy greater respect than managers who routinely do not deliver on their commitments.
- Produces good results—middle managers who pull their weight and add value to the company are respected and appreciated. Delivering results is a fundamental requirement for all middle

managers. Managers who produce poor results will not be well regarded by other managers or peers because they are not doing their part to contribute to corporate success. The exception to this is if the results are lacking due to conditions not under the middle manager's control.

- Is a pleasure or easy to work with—those managers with whom other staff members like to work will be perceived more favorably than those who are less fun and amiable. It is not important that a manager be an extrovert for him or her to be considered a pleasure to work with. Managers of all styles and philosophical persuasions can be easy to work with as long as they are accessible, interested, and helpful.

- Is knowledgeable and creative in their chosen field—managers and peers acknowledge and appreciate middle managers who know their stuff; this includes technical or specialized skills related to the department they manage. Furthermore, others in the organization will think well of middle managers who continue to learn and grow.

- Is an asset to the company—in most companies, only a small percentage of middle managers are outstanding assets to the company. When senior management considers a middle manager to be a great asset, he or she has demonstrated the ability and desire to contribute to the organization in a variety of ways. He or she will tend to be a manager who could successfully manage most departments or projects.

When people say that a manager has a bad reputation, they are saying that he or she

- Can't be trusted—perhaps he or she has abused confidences or burned someone in the past.
- Does not follow through on commitments—he or she has let people down.
- Does not get the job done when others do—his or her results are disappointing.

- Is in some way difficult to work with—he or she is not a team player.
- Does not have the right skills or aptitude—he or she lacks creativity or technical expertise.
- Is not an important contributor—he or she does not make a difference.

You probably will find it difficult and uncomfortable to take the steps necessary to learn about the reputation you have established in your organization. However, it would be even more undesirable to have no idea how others perceive you.

Middle managers can use three possible approaches to discover their reputation. The first, and easiest, approach is to ask. This method will work in environments where honest and open feedback is available.

Middle managers should also try the second approach, which is observation, particularly if the first approach does not yield full or truthful information. Many peers, managers, and team members will not feel comfortable being candid about their thoughts.

If the first two approaches fail to provide you with the necessary information, then try the third approach, which is to use an objective third party. Managers who need to use the third approach will often have a reputation that makes people reluctant and guarded with their feedback. In addition, middle managers in higher-level positions receive less honest feedback than their colleagues at lower levels do. Some people will be reluctant, for example, to tell a vice president about areas in which he or she needs to improve. Middle managers should be aware that it is going to be harder to get useful and helpful feedback as they progress up the ladder in their organization. This is unfortunate, because everyone needs good feedback to perform his or her best.

Let's look more closely at each of these three approaches.

Approach 1: Ask

An effective way for you to determine your reputation is to ask peers, managers, and team members. This, of course, works best if you have trusting and collaborative relationships that allow for open and honest communication. The questions that you ask and how you ask them are also important.

You may choose to meet with people one-to-one, but this approach is only going to yield accurate results in the most open and trusting work environments.

A sample form you can use to solicit feedback can be downloaded for free at www.lisahaneberg.com on the High-Impact Middle Management page. Ask your peers, managers, and team members to fill out this form and return it to you. You can choose to have the form returned directly to you, or to another person if you think this will help people be more open and honest. Ask for a response within five days, and encourage respondents to be open and honest. Compile the responses. Notice the trends and the relative rankings. Though respondents may not feel comfortable answering questions in a derogatory manner, the ranking and ratings will reveal which of the managerial traits are of the most concern. For example, if a manager is not reliable, chances are good that respondents will rank this trait toward the bottom, or 7, in most of the returned forms. The completed survey shown in example 4-1 represents real feedback given to a middle manager. The scores have all been averaged.

The overall interpretation of the feedback from this survey that this particular middle manager should arrive at is that she is very well regarded and respected by the folks who participated. This group sees her as an extremely results-oriented and highly productive manager. These are very positive scores. However, even with positive scores such as these, there will likely be one or two areas in which you need to improve. This middle manager's results are no exception.

First, it is clear that developing relationships is a relative weakness for this manager and may even be a potential future derailing factor. Related to this is her tendency to judge others and come across as too blunt and direct. These criticisms are all related to how this middle manager works with others. It is also apparent that she needs to be more cognizant of how she comes across to others and how she talks about other people.

It is likely that this middle manager has been battling these weaknesses throughout her career. Without this feedback, it is more likely that these problem areas could become more severe and begin affecting her career. It is also quite interesting that this middle manager scored no points in part 3 of example 4-1 under the option "can get emotional."

Example 4-1. Middle Management Survey for: Mr./Ms. Middle Manager

Please answer the survey openly and honestly. I am interested in learning the good, the bad, and the ugly. I consider this tool to be a part of my overall development plan and value your feedback. Please return the completed survey to me by next Monday. Thank you!

Part 1: Middle Management Qualities and Traits

For each trait listed, indicate whether this particular trait is a strength of mine or a weakness, or somewhere in the middle. If a weakness, please do not hesitate to point this out. Please also rank these traits from 1–7, 1 being the trait I am strongest in and 7 the trait that is the greatest weakness for me.

Middle Management Quality/Trait	Strength	Average	Weakness	Rank
Timely in regard to work and projects	xxxxxx			4.25
Reliable	xxxxxx			3.75
Easy to work with, even when times are difficult	xxxxx	x		4.5
Acts quickly and follows up	xxxxxx			3.25
Results oriented	xxxxxx			1.25
Skilled manager	xxxxx	x		3.5
Builds and maintains relationships	x	xxxxx		6.75

Part 2: Open-Ended Questions

Complete the following questions, providing as many specifics as possible.

Share a time when this manager let someone down at work. *Too quick to pass judgment. Cannot think of a time. Only minor things (4).*

Share the most important contribution this manager has made to the organization in the last year. *Department workflow. Developing good processes. Elevated the level of her department (3).*

What has been his or her greatest failure in the last year? *Don't know. Qualities of all her employees not up to standard (3).*

How well do you believe this manager represents you and your interests? *Very well. Always honest. Always supportive. For the most part excellent but there may also be times when she gives an opinion about me that is inaccurate and is not helpful.*

Do you consider this manager highly productive, satisfactorily productive, or below average in productivity? Highly productive (5).

What do people like most and least about working with this manager?

Most: *Knows her stuff. Is always there for you. Thoroughness and dependability. Smart, quick, funny. Gets things done. Keeps people focused and honest.*

Least: *Can be very matter-of-fact, lacking empathy. Afraid you may not measure up in her eyes. Bluntness. Sometimes abrupt and too direct.*

Part 3: Descriptive Phrases

Each section below contains four phrases. Spread 100 points across the four phrases, giving more points to those phrases that are more descriptive of this manager and his or her performance and fewer points to those phrases that are less descriptive. You can, for example, give 50 points to the first two phrases and 0 points to the other two, or give 30 points to one while giving the others, 20, 10, and 40 points, respectively.

Management style:	100 Points Total
Teamwork oriented	31
Values individual initiative and creativity	31
Values security and predictability	11
Hard-driving competitiveness and focus on results	27
This manager is thought to be:	100 Points Total
Trustworthy	28
Reliable	26
A good partner	22
Responsible	24
When times get tough/busy, this manager:	100 Points Total
Plans well and is organized	56
Can get emotional	0
Represents the needs of his or her team members well	44
Can get overwhelmed	0

Though this means that she keeps her cool, it also relates to her tendency to lack empathy and be too matter-of-fact.

As these results show, even very strong and well-respected middle managers will benefit from learning more about the reputation they have developed in the organization. Paying attention to relative rankings and reoccurring themes will help you to better understand your strengths and weaknesses.

Approach 2: Observe

Another way that middle managers can determine their reputation is to observe how others interact with and around them. Peers, managers, and team members will communicate and respond in ways that reflect their feelings. Middle managers should take note of these aspects:

- Inclusivity versus exclusivity—managers held in high regard will find themselves invited to participate in more conversations and meetings to discuss emerging issues than middle managers who do not enjoy as positive a reputation.
- Project assignments—highly regarded middle managers will find that senior managers ask them to lead or take part in important projects.
- Confidential information—all middle managers are privy to some proprietary company information. There are many conversations, however, that take place about new ideas, potential deals, and upcoming changes in the organization. Managers learn who does not keep confidences or likes to spread gossip. If you find yourself excluded from sensitive information, your reputation may be suffering.
- What happens in tough situations—results-oriented middle managers will be the logical go-to people when something needs to be done quickly and well. Managers who have failed to meet deadlines or produce results in the past will not be on the top of the list of folks to go to when opportunity or problems strike.
- Confidence in goals and deadlines—middle managers known for delivering on their goals and deadlines will find that others have confidence in their work and plans.

- Collaboration and cooperation from peers—peers and managers will treat middle managers who have been great partners more warmly and collaboratively than they do those who have not been good partners. Peers are also more likely to look out for those with whom they have established a positive and strong reputation.
- Career progression—middle managers can get an indication about their reputation by looking at how their career has progressed. This includes the promotions they have received as well as those that they wanted but did not receive. Middle managers who fail to receive promotions should assume there is probably something about their reputations that needs improvement.
- Feedback and performance evaluations—middle managers should notice what their manager does and does not say when providing feedback or explaining a performance evaluation. Which skills or responsibilities does the manager, without hesitation, say are the middle manager's strengths? Which responsibilities does the manager talk about using qualifiers or less favorable terms?

Managers who notice how others treat them should be able to get a feel for the reputations they have within the organization. One caution: Inclusion and participation based on a person's job or functional expertise are also required. The chief financial officer must provide input on finances, the physicist will take part in projects involving physics, and the captain needs to answer questions about navigation. When evaluating reputation, it is important to separate interactions and inclusion initiated because of one's position from other situations. Senior managers ask their valued middle managers to join in a wide variety of discussions and projects and include them early on when problems arise.

Approach 3: Use a Facilitator or Third Party

If you do not want to use approaches 1 and 2, or have tried them without success, you might want to enlist help from an objective third party. In many companies, this is a regular and normal practice. Some organizations have a corporate psychologist on staff or executive coaches who help senior and middle managers discover and improve their reputations.

Other organizations use human resources generalists or management development trainers to meet this need. Depending on the situation, an objective third party can use surveys, interviews, and observation to help you determine how to improve your effectiveness.

Another objective method that many companies use is 360-degree feedback instruments. These surveys are often chosen because they collect and compare information from the person (a self-assessment) as well as from his or her manager(s), peers, and employees. Most 360-degree feedback instruments have questions that measure the middle manager's reputation. These feedback instruments, however, are only as good as the data that go into them and the follow-up that results from them. They are most useful if you can get several peers, team members, and managers to complete the surveys and then positively and proactively respond to the feedback you receive.

Middle managers interested in learning what their reputations are in an organization can use any of these approaches. Great managers do what others don't or won't. Many managers never bother to think about how others see them or if they have a derailing factor getting in the way of their success. Middle managers who take the time and expend the energy to discover their reputations will experience, at the very least, an "aha moment" and, at best, a breakthrough. High-impact middle managers know their strengths and weaknesses and use this knowledge to grow and improve.

Case Study

Art had applied for two promotions and received neither. One was an internal support position in which he would interact with many other departments. When managers from other departments found out that Art had applied for this promotion, several expressed their concerns. They didn't want to work with him. Though he was highly qualified, he did not have the most important qualification: demonstrated ability and experience developing and maintaining positive work relationships. The hiring manager told him the truth. He was not going to get the position because he had a reputation for being difficult to work with and had burned bridges with internal customers over the last year. Until he fixed these problems, his career would go nowhere.

When faced with a significant derailing factor that affects their careers, many managers crumble. High-impact middle managers, however, use this situation as an opportunity to create a new definition of success. They look at what can be improved because they realize that success and accolades will naturally follow as a result of their being an outstanding partner with whom to work. Many managers find that they can repair burned bridges and reestablish credibility by consistently being collaborative and productive. It can be hard to deal with harsh feedback, but not doing so can permanently derail your career.

How to Assess Your Team's Reputation within the Organization

The human resources (HR) team at ABC Company was well regarded and enjoyed high levels of participation in most of the company's major initiatives. Many departments viewed working with HR as a positive and worthwhile activity and felt that the HR team helped them manage their part of the business more effectively. And the HR team's members were proud of their accomplishments and took their role of supporting the organization seriously. The managers of other business units coveted these HR team members for open positions, and most team members experienced positive career moves every two years or so.

In contrast, the accounting department was known as being inflexible, inaccurate, and slow. Managers did not trust the numbers it produced and felt they had to clean up after its errors. The processes the accounting department's team members used and the way they conducted business made it more difficult for managers to manage their departments. Many individuals on the accounting team did not progress or receive promotions. Of the talented employees who joined the accounting team, many left within six months. The employees who stayed on the team were marginal performers. The situation was so bad that people in other departments often circumvented processes to avoid contact with the accounting department.

These two examples may seem extreme, but both are real and commonplace. Most middle managers would like to see their team regarded similarly to the HR team in this example and not like the accounting team. By taking the time to evaluate your team's reputation, you will have the information and starting point you need to begin the improvement process. All teams have the potential to be well-regarded high performers. Making sure that your team is making a positive contribution to the organization should be your top priority, because it will drive success, satisfaction, and results. To discover and define your team's reputation in the organization, you should

- Ask peers and managers.
- Observe and listen.
- Measure performance.
- Talk with team members.

Let's look more closely at each of these techniques.

Ask Peers and Managers

To assess the reputation of your team, you can ask many of the same questions you would use to determine your own reputation. For individuals and teams alike, reputations form around and center on similar questions: Can they be trusted? Do they deliver results? Are they positive to work with? Are they reliable? Are they responsive? To understand the answers to these questions, middle managers should regularly talk with their peers and managers, asking open-ended questions like these:

- In what ways does this department excel?
- In what ways does this department fail to meet expectations?
- If you were the manager, what improvements or changes would you make to this team?
- What is it like to work with this team?
- When was the last time you felt frustrated because of this team's performance or an interaction with team members?
- What is one change that would make working with this team more pleasurable?
- What goal or improvement initiative would be most worthwhile over the next year?
- What do others say about this team?

When a middle manager talks with his or her peers and manager about how to improve the team's performance, he or she will often get valuable information about how they currently regard the team. Discovering a team's reputation is not nearly as hard as determining one's own reputation.

Observe and Listen

Middle managers can also pick up information about their team's reputation by paying attention to verbal and nonverbal clues. In meetings, how do people refer to the team? When project managers assign tasks for a cross-functional project, is the team included begrudgingly or enthusiastically as an important contributor? Do people try to include team members or go around them to get their work done? It is common practice to see alternative systems and processes pop up for the sole purpose of not having to involve your particular department or team? If this happens, it should be a giant clue that your team suffers from a poor reputation. For example, with the accounting team mentioned above, several departments tracked their own data and created their own reports. A couple of departments found ways around the purchasing system to get the items they needed on time. Middle managers who make it a point to observe these activities can be more proactive in preventing needless duplications of work and improving their team's performance and reputation.

Measure Performance

Teams that meet their goals and produce results will often also have a positive reputation in the organization. Middle managers should know how their team is performing for many reasons, including understanding if the company sees the team as a positive contributor. The next section offers techniques for measuring team performance.

Talk with Team Members

Most team members know and sense how others in the organization regard their team. If the team is enjoying a positive reputation, its members will feel pride and satisfaction. If the team has a poor reputation, this will likely be a source of stress and frustration for its members. For middle managers, there are two significant advantages to asking the team's members about its reputation. First, managers will learn valuable and useful information that they can use to set goals and select improvement initiatives. Second, team members who talk about their performance are more likely to become part of the solution and improvement effort. And along with asking your team members' opinions, try to solicit their input and ideas for getting to the next level of performance and effectiveness.

How to Measure Your Team's Performance against Goals and Results

Along with understanding your team's reputation, you also need to measure its performance to establish the correct goals. This goes beyond knowing that everyone is working hard and doing their best to taking the time to measure throughput and results.

Often, a team is producing much more than the manager or the organization realizes. Sometimes the reverse is also true. Clearly defining current performance helps establish the starting point for all goals and initiatives. Many managers think of measuring performance as an undesirable and a low-value-added task. How mistaken these managers are! Team performance measures help middle managers gain the support and resources they need and make their jobs easier and more fruitful, as shown in the case study about Tim.

Case Study

Tim's predecessors had requested additional personnel to process the massive amounts of information that flowed through his department. But senior managers had turned down their requests and, in some cases, cut their resources. Tim could see the need for people to process the information more effectively and quickly, and he knew that he would need senior managers' support to dedicate resources in this area. He did something the managers before him had not: He measured performance and productivity. He determined that each employee spent more than 35 percent of his or her time on processing, and, that as a team, their efficiency was lower than desired. By dedicating personnel to the sole task of processing,

efficiencies would improve and overall personnel costs would decrease. Had Tim not measured current performance and produced
the data to back up his assertions, it is unlikely that he would have
found support for creating new positions.

High-impact middle managers make it a priority to know and continually measure their team's performance. They do so by establishing ongoing systems and practices for updating and communicating throughput
and results. They know the key financial and nonfinancial metrics that
matter most. To determine the correct things to measure, ask yourself
these questions:

1. What is the most important contribution that internal and external
    customers expect this team to make? Is the team meeting the expec-
    tations of internal and external customers?
2. What are the primary products and services produced by this team?
    What are the team's productivity and throughput related to these
    products and services?
3. Is the team meeting its goals? Why or why not?
4. How would this team's internal and external customers define the
    responsiveness and speed that they expect from this team? Is the
    team meeting expectations?
5. What major initiatives or projects is this team supporting? Are team
    members completing their project work on time and well?
6. What expectations exist about improving departmental processes
    and methods? Are team members taking the time and using initia-
    tive to improve how they do their work?

On the basis of the answers to these questions, you can begin to identify
the most important metrics to track. It is helpful to create a quick reference
sheet of several metrics, so that you can regularly review them with your
team members and managers (a tool for communicating metrics, called
the High-Impact Middle Management Playbook, is presented in chapter
5). Furthermore, middle managers who involve the team in measuring and
reporting on these metrics will improve their team members' connection,
empowerment, and ownership of the department's results and success.

Case Study

Each year during the budgeting process, senior managers challenged Corky to lower the HR department's head count. This was always a frustrating process because she knew that, if anything, she needed more help. Although the company was small, it hired and then laid off many seasonal employees each year. Corky measured the throughput and results of the HR team. The numbers were enlightening and helpful. The department was recruiting, hiring, processing, evaluating, and terminating employees at a rate more typical of a company four times its size. The usual ratio of one HR person for every 100 employees would not work for this department. Corky did need more help and, with good information and measurements, she was able to get it.

How to Communicate Current Performance Findings to Managers and Team Members

Some middle managers take the time to measure performance but then fail to communicate performance to their team members or their managers. Management is a social act. If you collect information but then do nothing with it, you are not truly managing. Measurements can only be useful when managers and team members discuss, respond to, and use measurement information to improve performance in the future. To communicate current performance, middle managers should

- Meet regularly with their manager to review performance. At this meeting, you should come prepared with a list of current performance measures, a summary of those things that are going well, concerns, and your action plan for addressing the concerns. This meeting can be brief, as short as 30 minutes. Middle managers should meet with their managers on at least a monthly basis. During peak production periods or major initiatives, meetings should occur more often.
- Discuss team performance and metrics at every team meeting. Ask open-ended questions to clarify concerns or to collect team members' ideas for resolving issues regarding throughput

or results. Speak about concerns and performance shortfalls in a matter-of-fact way that communicates to team members that performance needs to improve but that this is not something personal.

- Post team measurements in a visible way. Ensure the team updates key performance measures regularly. Each team should have three to five fundamental deliverables that are most important. For example, the human resource team might track hiring accuracy and short-term turnover.

- Use information about current performance levels when planning future initiatives or setting goals. Projects and initiatives will be more successful if the team's strengths and weaknesses are accounted for and considered in their planning.

- Be sure to celebrate excellent team performance, major milestones, and accomplishments. Share these important performance achievements with peers and the rest of the organization.

Communicating current team performance enables managers and team members to react and begin the process of celebration or improvement. Most middle managers do not talk about team performance enough with their teams or managers. The many rewards of regular and open conversations about metrics include higher manager confidence, higher team morale, and better results.

When you understand the reputation you have in an organization, the reputation of your team, and their current performance metrics, you arm yourself with powerful information that will aid in planning, goal setting, and improvement initiatives. High-impact middle managers perform a reality check by practicing habits and employing methods that ensure they are aware of their work environment. In time, these habits and methods will become second nature and a normal part of your middle management practices.

Chapter 5

Using the High-Impact Middle Management Playbook to Facilitate Peak Performance

In sports, the goals are clear. Well-conceived and clearly communicated plays determine what each player does. Objectives are clarified during practice sessions, and each team member's performance is reviewed in detail after each game. Every player knows his or her stats and those of the team. Skill and results determine each team member's position and play time. Like great coaches, high-impact middle managers use planning, measurement, and communication skills to create performance targets and improve team accountability, execution, and results.

Just as a sports team uses a playbook to develop strategy and refine its game plan, so too can high-impact middle managers use a similar tool to refine their management practices and facilitate attaining peak performance from themselves and their team. Using the High-Impact Middle Management Playbook will enable you to set goals, establish plans, and measure performance in less time than with more conventional methods. The result will be significant improvements in work completion, quality, and throughput.

The Playbook

In sports, teams need to respond quickly and plan well between each game. They do not have time for elaborate processes or cumbersome tracking mechanisms. The High-Impact Middle Management Playbook (see figure 5-1) uses the efficient and time-saving aspects of the playbooks used in sports and adds features that meet the needs of busy middle managers. (The playbook can be downloaded at www.lisahaneberg.com.) Elements of a typical sports playbook include

- the strategy for each game
- a list of regular plays organized by category
- strategies for communicating and exchanging plays with others
- detailed statistics on each player and the players on the opponent's team
- the strengths and weaknesses of the team and its opponents.

The High-Impact Middle Management Playbook contains measures, indicators, and lists that many businesses track and value. It is important that you use this playbook only as a starting point. The playbook will be most useful when middle managers customize it to meet the needs of their departments. Its elements include

- descriptions of priorities and approaching projects
- short-term and long-term goals
- detailed metrics on the key financial and nonfinancial measures for the team
- ongoing work productivity statistics
- space for updates on work projects or tasks
- ways of optimizing work flow
- a list of concerns and barriers facing the team.

The playbook is an invaluable tool that will help you focus your time and energy on the tasks that will have the greatest impact on your team's results. It provides a snapshot of current team performance, priorities, and work assignments. Let's consider a detailed description of each section of the playbook shown in figure 5-1.

Priorities and Upcoming Projects

This section should include a brief list of future projects or initiatives that team members should consider and begin preparing for when planning their work. For example, if you work for a company that experiences

Figure 5-1. The High-Impact Middle Management Playbook

Ongoing Work		Status		Key Metrics		Current Performance	Priorities and Upcoming Projects
Short-Term Goals				Long-Term Goals			
							Concerns & Barriers
Task	Owner	Deadline		Task	Owner	Deadline	
							Productivity Questions: Why are we doing this? What difference will it make? Is there a better action to take? Is there an easier way? Are the right people involved? Does it improve results?

seasonal highs and lows, this section can be used to remind team members of important launch dates for busy times.

Short-Term and Long-Term Goals

Short-term goals are those your team will complete in the next one to six months. Long-term goals should mirror or support those listed in the strategic plan. Well-written goals include time frames, owners of tasks, and expected results. Reviewing both short-term and long-term goals on a regular basis helps your team stay aligned and able to meet today's needs and support the company's vision for the future. Other sections of the playbook should include tasks that support the goals listed here.

Key Financial and Nonfinancial Team Metrics

Each team should have a set of metrics that it collects, reviews, and reports periodically. These metrics measure how well the team is doing relative to the fundamental contributions it has been asked to make to the company. For a marketing team, for example, the metrics could include customer acquisition costs, the return-on-investment (ROI) for marketing campaigns, and exposure in the marketplace. If you are not already tracking these types of data, you should start because this information will help you stay abreast of performance and enable you to notice trends and emerging problems.

Ongoing Work Productivity

Each department has ongoing work that is important to track. Often this work will consume a significant portion of your team's time and resources. Examples of this type of work include processing checks, answering customer calls, processing new employees, maintaining systems, and supporting field operations. In this section of the playbook, you should list two or three of the most important ongoing products or services and describe how the team will track productivity. The items in this section will probably not change much from week to week, but productivity will vary with time.

Work Projects and Tasks

This portion of the playbook is the most dynamic and offers the clearest and quickest benefit to middle managers. The tasks that your team needs to complete are listed, along with the deadlines and owners for each task. As your team completes tasks, you can cross out these tasks in the playbook or leave them listed to help team members communicate the status of their work. Some managers will prefer to complete one playbook each week and keep previous copies in their day planner. Others may choose to keep one master playbook.

Work Flow Optimization

Middle managers use the playbook to track work against current and emerging priorities. By reviewing the playbook often and asking yourself questions about how you are using your resources, you can ensure that your team is producing at its best. Middle managers should also recognize and plan for short periods of high or low work demands by adjusting assignments or bringing in short-term help.

Concerns and Barriers

Listing concerns and barriers is critical to keeping you and your team members focused on resolving problems that could have an impact on throughput. Throughout the day and week, the middle manager fills this section with the normal challenges of running a business. As he or she crosses each entry off the list, it is a sign that work is flowing productively again. This section, more than any other, highlights high-impact middle management work in action!

Communicating the Playbook

A sports team uses its playbook faithfully. It is the central tool for communicating priorities and progress to the team. Producing consistent wins takes teamwide communication and participation.

This approach is not as common in business—though it should be. During the development and launch of Black & Decker's DeWalt line, product teams met frequently to discuss status, priorities, and their game plan. They also took time to celebrate successes along the way. Sometimes the team congratulated the engineers for creating a new and better feature. Other times, the marketing folks won praise for a well-timed coup in the marketplace.

Middle managers in any industry can use the High-Impact Middle Management Playbook in the same manner. Management is a social act, and the playbook is an excellent way to facilitate communication among you and your supervisors, team members, peers, and managers. The playbook is an organic tool, which should change to represent the current priorities and needs of your department. Middle managers should have their playbook with them at all meetings and review it at the beginning of each workday. Those who use a day planner for appointments should insert their playbook in their binders for easy reference. High-technology middle managers who prefer BlackBerries or laptops can load their playbook into their favorite device. By reviewing each section of the playbook at team meetings, middle managers can get input from team members on items to change or add, as well as gain understanding of and commitment to their priorities. This practice will also provide an opportunity for team members to ask questions, express concerns, identify barriers, and ask for necessary support.

How to Use the Playbook

You can begin using the High-Impact Middle Management Playbook by filling out each section and sharing it with your managers and team members to get input. If you do not currently have team metrics, you can take a few minutes to think about what they should be or hold a team meeting to discuss metrics as a group. Both long-term and short-term goals come from yearly plans. Middle managers who are not presently creating a departmental plan can use the tutorial at the end of this chapter.

Update the playbook daily, weekly, or as needed. Take it to all meetings. Information shared at meetings often fits into the upcoming projects or concerns and barriers sections. You will want to keep these and other sections current to get the most benefit from using the playbook.

Use the playbook as a platform for team update meetings. Revise and redistribute copies after each meeting so all your team members understand the plan and the action items for which they are responsible. Share the playbook with the peers who work most closely with your team. Doing so will create greater understanding, generate support, and improve relationships. The playbook is an excellent communication tool.

Middle managers can download the full-size version of the High-Impact Middle Management Playbook at www.lisahaneberg.com; follow the "High-Impact Middle Management" links. Finding a size and format that is easiest to use and maintain is an important part of using the playbook to track and improve team performance.

Customizing the Playbook

Middle managers should customize their playbooks to suit their needs. The playbook is most useful when it captures the daily and weekly concerns of the middle manager. The intent of a playbook is to provide a quick reference for middle managers and their team members that, when used, helps the manager and team stay aligned and on track. Throughout the day, you should carry the playbook and update sections as needed. Examples of sections that you may want to add to the playbook include

- meetings to schedule or prepare for
- team meeting discussion topics
- phone numbers of important contacts
- questions for peers or managers
- areas needing research or analysis
- action items that you have requested from others.

By customizing your playbook, you will optimize the effectiveness and relevance of this tool and management practice. Middle managers can tailor the playbook to meet their needs and complement their preferred planning style.

Creating a Departmental Strategic Plan: A Tutorial

Depending on your company's size and culture, you may or may not receive the training and coaching needed to create a departmental strategic plan. A departmental plan includes a departmental vision aligned with the corporate vision; three to five objectives that support corporate objectives; and goals, projects, and initiatives that produce these objectives. Each company may use slightly different terminology, but don't worry about that. The exact names are not important. The importance of a plan is that it tells the middle manager and his or her team:

- why they exist and the contribution they are expected to make to the corporation
- their priorities and most important initiatives
- the plan for delivering the promised results.

To get to this point, you, as a middle manager, need to learn and understand the corporate strategic plan and answer several questions about long-term and short-term needs, changes, and opportunities. The following questions can be used to help brainstorm needs and considerations for a departmental strategic plan.

Long term—one to three years:

- Based on the strategic plan (developed by senior management), what will be the purpose of this function over the next several years?
- How will the work change?
- What skills and resources will my team members need? How will these skills be developed in time to meet tomorrow's challenges?
- What changes should occur today to meet strategic goals?
- What are the major milestones to observe/strive for over the next three years?
- What's coming down the pike, and will it need attention?
- Will a different kind of management be required to produce different results? How should new skills be acquired and put into place?
- What is my department doing today that does not support the strategic direction?
- What should my team be working on to ensure that it is being aligned with future goals and initiatives?
- What do my team members need to know about the future direction?

Midterm—this year:

- What does the company expect my team to accomplish this year? What are my team's deliverables? What are my team's current strengths and weaknesses?
- What will it take to deliver? What resources are required in the areas of people, roles, systems, processes, and projects? What should be included in the business plan and budget to achieve objectives?
- What changes will occur during the next year? Does my team have a clear implementation plan for change defined and in place?
- Does my team need to realign roles or processes to fulfill this year's business plan? Will my staff need new skills?

- What are the most important monthly and quarterly milestones? What business processes are required to ensure that my department is focused on achieving these milestones?
- Are there decisions that need to be made to enable the team's success?

Short term—this month:

- What is the work plan for the month? What key results does my team need to deliver? Can it get all the work done? How will I communicate progress on the work plan?
- What are the barriers to my team's success? What is the plan for ensuring that barriers are defined and removed?
- Which metrics provide the best information about the team's productivity and results?
- What meetings should I schedule, plan, and lead to facilitate good communication, creativity, coordination, and/or problem solving?
- How should I spend my time to make the greatest impact?
- What coaching and/or development should I seek?
- How will I ensure that others make timely decisions affecting the team?
- What is my plan for coaching and developing my staff?
- What worries my team members, managers, and peers most? With whom should I talk about these concerns? Is there anything I have been putting off?

Weekly and daily:

- What does my team need to accomplish today or this week, and what's the plan for ensuring that it all gets done?
- What are the problems and barriers getting in the way of productivity? Who should be working on these barriers? How can I remove barriers today?
- With whom do I need to communicate today?
- How should I spend my time today?
- Have I prepared for today's meetings?

These questions, though a bit overwhelming, will help you brainstorm about the type of information needed for the departmental strategic plan. Middle managers should be able to answer each question. The rough data will help you create the vision, objectives, and goals for your departmental plan. Though formats and terms differ from company to company, here are definitions for each part of the departmental strategic plan:

- *Vision:* The vision is a short statement, one to three sentences long, that states the main purpose for your team and the contribution it makes to the corporation. Example: The marketing department serves as the voice of the company in the marketplace. Marketing creates and conveys the company's brands, products, and services in ways that maximize market share, revenues, and customer satisfaction. The work of the marketing department is fundamental to the company's revenue generation and goals for market growth.

- *Objectives:* Most departments should have three to five broad targets covering each major area or function within the department. Each objective should define the target, the timeline for completion, and the measures of success. Example: Utilize the web to improve knowledge of the product, market reach, and to facilitate revenue generation. In the next year, implement two or three web-based tools or products that generate revenue at an ROI of at least 10:1 (that is, they generate $10 in revenue for every $1 spent).

- *Goals:* Most department plans contain two to five goals for each objective. Goals may be initiatives or projects. Goals must be specific, measurable, and have deadlines. Example: Develop and implement a plan for training distributors and wholesalers using web-based technology. Complete 40 training sessions with an average attendance of 15 persons and an average ROI of 10:1 or better by the end of the year.

After creating a rough plan, you should review the complete plan to ensure that it is realistic. Departmental plans should be challenging and represent the work that can be accomplished when the team is highly productive. It is common to see departmental plans that are not practical or possible. Middle managers who create plans that contain too many projects or initiatives are setting their teams up for failure and frustration. If the objectives or projects are being requested by senior management, it may be necessary to negotiate the plan. Often, it is a question of people and resources. Many middle managers do not even bother to stand up for their teams when they are being asked to do more than is possible. Middle managers should do any or all of the following to ensure that their plan is robust and doable:

- Challenge conventional thinking. Is the plan really impossible? What if the department were reorganized or realigned?
- Negotiate the work. Are there projects or tasks that could be discontinued to allow new and higher-priority work to be completed? Be clear about what the department can and cannot do.
- Ask for more resources. Are new projects or initiatives important enough to warrant additional and dedicated resources?
- Ask the team. The team members may offer great ideas for how the work can get done. They often know of ways to save resources and reduce waste.
- Ask peers for their ideas and input. Do they think the plan is unrealistic? What would they do if this were their plan?

Once the middle manager and senior managers negotiate and agree to the plan, the middle manager should communicate it to all team members. Then the High-Impact Middle Management Playbook picks up where the departmental plan leaves off and serves as a daily tool to enable middle managers to stay on track with their plan.

Day-to-Day Execution

Chapter 6

Mucky-Muck Obstructions: Navigating the Corporate Obstacle Course

Middle managers link teams, systems, and processes together to produce results. This requires working with many different people and under varied circumstances, which, in turn, can produce conflict, contradiction, and chaos—also known as mucky-muck. Mucky-muck causes a great deal of teeth-gnashing frustration, often reflected in comments such as:

- Why is it so hard to get anything done around here?
- Why did I waste my time?
- Why wasn't I told that up front?
- It takes forever to get a decision made in this company.
- She and I just don't see eye to eye. I'll sit this one out.

Dealing with some mucky-muck is an inevitable part of any job; however, unresolved mucky-muck can quickly turn to quicksand that mires productivity, morale, and positive communication. To be successful as a middle manager, you need to be part investigator, part mind reader, and part magician. Knowing how to navigate through corporate mucky-muck is an essential middle management skill.

Sixteen Variations of Mucky-Muck

The first step in getting through the mucky-muck is to recognize what it looks like. Like various strains of a virus, all mucky-muck shares some common elements. Mucky-muck is generally rooted in people's emotional and defensive reactions to feelings of personal censure or self-doubt. Other forms of mucky-muck share an element of process, structure, or role getting in the way of common sense. Every work environment will breed and support different kinds of mucky-muck. Let's look at the 16 forms that are the most common in many companies.

Variation 1: Miscommunication

Lou wondered why it was taking Mike so long to respond to his request for a few cost projections. He didn't know that Mike was upset because he thought that Lou was trying to usurp a portion of his territory. This was, in fact, not the case; but Mike responded emotionally to the perceived threat and thus had no incentive to help Lou.

Middle managers spend a surprisingly large amount of time clearing up confusion or hurt feelings that arise from miscommunication. Emails are one of the biggest miscommunication generators because it is hard for the recipient to interpret the intent and tenor of brief, written messages. To reduce the likelihood of miscommunication, make requests clear and specific, and provide examples to illustrate your meaning. Regularly talk in person or on the phone and resist the urge to assume that you know what others are thinking. To avoid this type of mucky-muck, it is best to err on the side of overcommunicating with peers and team members.

Variation 2: Politics

Jim and his managers met with Jake to share their plan for the coming year. They knew they needed to get Jake's support before they presented their plan to the CEO. If the CEO knew that Jake supported the plan, he would be less likely to reject it. It often worked best to have Jake share the plan with the CEO one-to-one to address the CEO's concerns before the management team met with him. Although it took a few extra steps, this was the way Jim was best able to implement important changes.

The posturing and maneuvering that occur within a group or company is its politics. Nonpolitical managers, like Jim, are often forced to play politics to get things done. Gaining, keeping, or controlling power is often the motivation for politics. Managers who are political often think in hierarchical terms and show a preference for exclusivity. Though politics is an inevitable part of many business environments, middle managers can reduce the negative impact of politics by learning the unwritten rules about how decisions are made. It is also important to ensure that you do not let concerns about status, ego, or self-preservation get in the way of your productivity. It is best to focus on those actions that will benefit work relationships and results.

Variation 3: Passing the Buck and Pointing Fingers

Harry's boss asked him why one of his teams was short several staff members and was unable to meet its productivity goals. Harry had a problem supervisor who was causing people to walk off the job with no notice; but instead of being open about this, he blamed the problem on the human resources department. Harry knew that this problem's root cause was the particular manager, and that he had neglected to do anything about it, hoping the situation would improve without his intervention.

Every day, middle managers face tough questions about their teams, processes, and results. If they suffer from low self-esteem and confidence, more often than not they will try to make sure they don't appear to be wrong or at fault in front of others. This may manifest itself in blaming their peers, managers, or, worse yet, subordinates for problems. As one can imagine, this form of mucky-muck breeds more obstacles, such as miscommunication and burned bridges. Middle managers who encounter this type of mucky-muck should take the initiative to facilitate discussions where the facts and various perspectives can be conveyed. It is best to do this while maintaining a neutral and professional demeanor and by focusing on solving the problem (not on how this situation arose).

Variation 4: Undiscussables

Several members of the senior management team drove back to the office after an all-day off-site strategic planning meeting. As was typical, the meeting had been fine but lacked any real value. The CEO and president had asked for input, but they had only received a watered-down version of the managers' ideas, concerns, and complaints. Three fears had kept the managers from being honest about what they thought were the major problems in the company. First, they did not want to upset the CEO or president and make the rest of the day (and week) more difficult. Second, the managers did not feel comfortable saying they disagreed with some decisions that had been made by their bosses. Third, they feared that discussing their personal frustrations could damage their careers and standing with the executives.

"Undiscussable" topics may include feelings and opinions about the company, the work, and individual employees and customers. These undiscussables are common knowledge, such as the incompetent boss who got his promotion through nepotism or the low salary scale that erodes morale and makes it impossible to retain the best employees, but they are never verbalized or publicly acknowledged. Undiscussables are those issues that people are thinking about but that are too delicate, embarrassing, uncomfortable, or scary to discuss openly in a group setting. The problem is that these issues are being discussed by staff at the water cooler, over lunch, and behind closed doors.

There are two ways for middle managers to ensure that undiscussables don't get in the way of how they manage and lead. The first and more direct approach is to acknowledge the undiscussable. As a middle manager, you have the responsibility to be open and objective. This includes having the courage and conviction to take on tough topics. It is unlikely that you will lose your job or have your stature lowered for being open and honest (as long as it is constructive). Most undiscussables should be handled using the direct approach.

The second and less direct approach is to facilitate having certain individuals bring up the topic in the most palatable way. For example, a president once asked a particular board member to attend a planning meeting because he was certain the CEO would be more responsive to ideas offered by that board member. Granted, this approach smacks a little of politics, but in some work environments it might be the most effective way for you to get results.

Variation 5: Disorganization

When Sally joined the company, it took her two months to sort through her predecessor's piles of paper and disorganized files to discover what was going on. Meanwhile, she missed several deadlines she was unaware even existed. There was no work plan or project calendar to reference. Middle managers who take over a new function often face this form of muckymuck. When misplaced data, buried files, or rarely seen desktops get in the way of completing a task, the work environment suffers from disorganization. Disorganization can affect an individual, a team, or an entire function or company. Middle managers can get a handle on disorganization by creating a team event around getting organized. Have a Friday afternoon desk cleanout event, or a once-a-month organizing extravaganza. What you don't want to do is let getting organized wait—there may be something important and urgent on the bottom of one of those stacks of paper.

Variation 6: Learned Helplessness

Tim was struck by how listless, compliant, and dependent several of his employees were. They seemed like intelligent and dedicated people, but they did not demonstrate an ability to think independently or be enthusiastic about the work. Tim learned that the previous two managers had discouraged initiative and rewarded those who were compliant. Many in his group thus demonstrated learned helplessness, which occurs when a person or group accepts a certain reality based on previous experiences or information. In the corporate environment, learned helplessness is common, and it is most often faced by middle managers who take over managing a team of people who have previously not performed well. Learned helplessness can be unlearned when the middle manager communicates and clarifies expectations and roles, and then follows up with training and reinforcement of the new expectations. By asking employees for their input (versus being directive), middle managers can help raise the expectations the employees have of themselves.

Variation 7: Hidden Agendas

Debbie called a meeting with the marketing and product managers to share her idea for a new product. Though her concept was interesting, the managers could not help but wonder about her real motivation for the proposed change. Perhaps what she really wanted was for her group to produce the new product because she thought it would be more exciting and interesting than the product they were supposed to launch next year.

Middle managers often work with people who have hidden agendas. These hidden agendas become a problem when they get in the way of others doing their jobs or relating in a genuine way. The reason a person acts a certain way or makes a particular decision is often a mystery. However, hidden agendas often revolve around power, being right, getting ahead, looking good to the boss, covering up a failure, or gaining support for a pet project. Hidden agendas can often be revealed by asking open-ended questions about the intent, benefits, and evolution of the idea or project. A middle manager's objective is not necessarily to eliminate hidden agendas but rather to understand them so that he or she can make a well-informed decision.

Variation 8: Long-Term Alliances

Corky had done her homework. Her detailed and well-researched proposal recommended changing a major employee benefit vendor. Making the change would save the company money and would provide better service to its employees. It seemed to be a win-win situation. Little did Corky know that the current vendor, which charged premium rates and provided only average service, had a long-standing personal relationship with the CEO. Sure enough, what should have been a foolproof proposal failed miserably. Because middle managers interact with managers at all levels of the organization, it is inevitable that they will encounter this breed of mucky-muck. Old relationships or alliances can thwart productivity when they get in the way of sound business decisions or make the workplace dysfunctional. The best defense against being blindsided by long-term alliances is to ask questions early in the project planning process.

Variation 9: Burned Bridges

Lou was mortified. He had accidentally sent an email message disparaging a coworker to that very coworker! Though Lou apologized, he could not reverse the damage done to the relationship. As a middle manager, you may need to deal with burned bridges—whether your own or those of others in your department. Burned bridges get in the way of future communication and collaboration. The problem can get worse when other employees in the department get embroiled in the messy matter. To prevent burning a bridge with a peer or manager, never say or write anything that you would not feel comfortable repeating to that person directly. In particular, resist the urge to send inflammatory or emotional emails.

Variation 10: Clashes in Style

Dana and Sally were intelligent and dedicated managers who could not communicate effectively with each other. They conversed with each other in patronizing and disrespectful tones. However, when they worked with other people, everything was fine. The breakdown only occurred when they interacted with each other. Why did Dana and Sally have this problem? Their communication and behavioral styles clashed so severely that they annoyed each other and were unable to communicate effectively. They also lacked mutual respect, a situation that often accompanies a clash in styles.

High-impact middle managers need to be part psychologist and part mediator when faced with employees or coworkers whose styles clash and get in the way of their working relationship. Unfortunately, this makes work more difficult for everyone who has to compensate for those individuals. If you focus on the task at hand and not on how the other person presents himself or herself, you will be more successful in dealing with clashes in style. Recognizing and being open about style differences will help disarm the power and magnitude of the clash.

Variation 11: Disempowerment

Jane was feeling overwhelmed and in danger of losing her job, and so she was not getting her work done on time. Her employees, on the other hand, had time and capacity to spare. In particular, Kathy had a strong background and work experience that could have helped Jane with several of the larger projects she was unable to complete on schedule. In fact, based on the scope of Kathy's job, at least one of the projects should have been her responsibility in the first place; but Jane chose to take it on herself because the work was interesting. Had Jane asked her to, Kathy could have done much of the work and planning; and the project would have been completed on time.

Disempowerment results in workload problems for the manager who is taking on more than he or she should. To recognize and reduce the effects of disempowerment, middle managers should periodically review roles and team member workloads with their manager and team. For each to-do item on your list, ask the question "Should I be doing this, or does it belong on someone else's list?"

Aside from the loss of productivity, there are other disadvantages to disempowerment. Middle managers who disempower their employees lessen their intrinsic motivation and job satisfaction. And disempowerment also causes role ambiguity, workflow disruptions, and miscommunication.

Variation 12: Contradictory Information

Mike was frustrated because he was not getting answers about why sales of third-party products had dropped dramatically from last year. Lou and Tim, the middle managers in charge of this revenue stream, were supposed to provide analysis and an action plan for getting back on track. The problem was that Tim and Lou did not see the significant drop that Mike did. In fact, some of their data suggested that sales had actually improved from the previous year. The accounting department was working on providing a new and more accurate report, but it was running into contradictions and inconsistencies in the data. Two months had passed, and Mike was worried that the opportunity to fix the situation would evaporate. Meanwhile, Lou and Tim weren't even convinced that a problem existed.

Middle managers spend countless hours trying to find and validate the information they use to make decisions. Working with contradictory information is frustrating and wastes precious time. Worse yet, incorrect information can cause major errors in judgment and decisions. Middle managers who ask questions about how information is collected and take the initiative to analyze important measurements within their areas of responsibility are less likely to be affected by contradictory information. It is rarely a good strategy to assume that no news is good news concerning fundamental business processes.

Variation 13: Duplication of Efforts

Todd talked to Jake about creating an auditing process to ensure that products were meeting customer expectations. Lilly, as part of her overall product planning and improvement responsibilities, was also working on a new auditing process. When she found out that Todd had gone to Jake with his idea for an auditing process, she asked Todd why he was working on it. Todd said that he saw a need and took it upon himself to put together a plan. He did not know that Lilly had planned to create and implement a similar process. Together, they eventually worked it out so only one process was developed; but in the interim, everyone's valuable time was wasted. It was also uncomfortable for Lilly, who felt as though Todd had taken initiative in her area of responsibility.

Middle managers' responsibilities often overlap, but duplications of effort are wasteful and disruptive to the organization. Sometimes, as in the example of Lilly and Todd, duplication occurs because of misinformation. Other times, duplications occur because one manager does not have confidence in another—a hidden agenda for sure! Peers who regularly get together to share projects and priorities are less likely to get tripped up by duplications of effort. In addition, middle managers should know and respect one another's roles and areas of responsibility.

Variation 14: Sticks-in-the-Mud

Charlie had been with the company a long time, and he remembered when it had been much smaller and easier to manage. Any time a new idea for automating information or processes came up, he would balk at the idea. He didn't believe that the company needed to go to such lengths. He believed that the methods of yesterday would serve the current organization just as well. Not all sticks-in-the-mud are long-term employees reminiscing about "the good old days"; however, they do share a dislike of change and are leery of new approaches. Middle managers who face this type of mucky-muck spend more time and energy enrolling others in efforts at change.

Sticks-in-the-mud can get in the way of progress and make implementing new ideas more difficult. Middle managers can deal with change-resistant people by frequently communicating the purpose, plan, and staff roles relative to the change. You need to make sure that all employees understand the change and the reasons for it. Much resistance is born out of misinformation. Ultimately, change-resistant employees should not be allowed to sabotage or get in the way of changes that have been agreed upon.

Variation 15: Group Defections

Ron and his management team made all the right comments when they participated in companywide training meetings. They even seemed positive and optimistic about announced changes. However, when they returned to their workplace, it was as if none of these conversations had taken place. The members of Ron's management team decided that they would do the work their own way and ignore any direction from the home office that they found unappealing. Together, they essentially defected from the overall management team and became their own separate entity. As a result, their division did not reflect the overall vision of the company, and employees who transferred to their unit from other departments did not do well.

Group defections are more common in corporate America than one would think, and they cause breaks in communication, work inefficiencies, and lower morale and employee satisfaction. Middle managers can eliminate group defections by ensuring that they spend time with each of their work teams and handle concerns and problems proactively. It is not enough to manage through emails and staff meetings. High-impact middle managers know what's going on in the groups they manage, because they spend quality time building formal and informal relationships and partnerships with each team and manager.

Variation 16: Sabotage

Deirdre knew it was not going to work. She had told the members of the management team before they implemented the new process that it would make her group less efficient and that they felt confused by the new procedures. Other groups had implemented the new automated pro-cess with few problems and had reduced processing times using the new system. Deirdre's manager, Bob, felt that she had caused the project to fail by disparaging the change to her team. She had practiced a form of subtle sabotage when she spoke negatively about the change to her em-ployees. She had even encouraged them to help her amass evidence to keep things the way they were.

Most middle managers have experienced sabotage at one time or an-other. The most common forms of sabotage are negative and inappropri-ate comments about changes or decisions that have been made. Sabotage harms productivity, communication, and morale. Middle managers can reduce the likelihood of sabotage by being highly visible and accessible during times of change and by closely monitoring change implementa-tion. Visibility will increase the manager's opportunity to observe and notice the subtle clues that a team member is not doing his or her part to support the change.

Summing Up

Do any of these forms of mucky-muck sound familiar? There is a practical reason for classifying these barriers as mucky-muck. Each represents weak, immature, or shortsighted behavior on the part of an individual, group, or company. Mucky-muck does not make sense—it just is. This is not to say that it does not matter or cause damage. In some work environments, the mucky-muck is so thick that it drives smart people away or causes them to fail. Studying these characterizations of corporate folly will help you tackle it. In addition, when called "mucky-muck," a ridiculous name, to be sure, its power dwindles. Like calling a seven-foot muscle builder "Tiny," calling these barriers mucky-muck lessens their ability to intimidate. Mucky-muck is inevitable, but you can have a significant impact on how much mucky-muck there is and how your staff responds to it.

Eleven Techniques for Navigating Mucky-Muck

Teams rely on their managers to cut through the mucky-muck and help them get their jobs done. Middle managers are most likely to face mucky-muck because they interact with more functions, levels, groups, and individuals than do others in the company. Once mucky-muck presents itself, you can reduce its power over your department and organization. High-impact middle managers have figured out how to best respond to mucky-muck so it does not get in the way of results. Let's look at 11 high-impact middle management techniques for navigating through the corporate mucky-muck.

Technique 1: Do the Right Homework

Jim and his team needed to come up with a strategic business plan for the coming year. They knew that senior management had several preconceived ideas about what the plan should look like. Rather than wasting their time creating a plan that only represented what they thought the priorities should be, they first sought to understand the senior managers' points of view, and then they developed their plan. Some might say this approach was faulty because it led to Jim and his team circumscribing their own ideas to those of senior management. Though this may be true, the team knew that the senior managers had already made up their minds about what they thought needed to happen. The team members knew that they could most help the organization by developing a plan that implemented senior management's ideas in the best possible way. In the end, they were able to influence several aspects of the plan much more than they would have had they not been sensitive to senior management's agendas.

As a middle manager, you will face situations like this on a regular basis. If there are strong opinions or relationships influencing a decision maker, it is best to do your homework and discover what they are before wasting too much time working in an opposite direction. Before starting a project, ask yourself, "Is there historical information that would be helpful to know? What are senior management's thoughts on this project? What approaches have been suggested in the past? Are there preferred vendors or partners that should be maintained?" There may be times when this added work and research is not necessary and unencumbered creative thinking is possible. However, it is always better to err on the side of being prepared and doing your homework.

Technique 2: Pick and Choose Your Battles

Ann knew that she was right about the benefits of changing to a different vendor and that she had presented a thorough case to her bosses. She felt the decision to turn down her proposal was not logical. She did not want to let go of her idea, but in the end she realized that it was not a battle worth fighting. The current vendor cost more and did not provide the high level of service that the proposed vendor would have; but overall, the service they did receive was satisfactory. Nothing terrible was going to happen if they kept the current vendor. There would be bigger and more important battles to fight another day, and Ann knew it was better to let this one go.

Middle managers often face the decision whether to hold firm and fight for what they think is right or accept another decision and move on. If you wage too many battles, you may end up commanding less respect in your organization. In addition, your message will seem watered-down and ineffective. Like the story of the boy who cried wolf, if you tout every proposal or idea as critically important, you will eventually find that the truly important projects will be ignored or seen as being unworthy of special consideration. High-impact middle managers know how to choose their battles and use their influence for maximum gain and consequence.

Technique 3: Focus Energy Where It Will Count

Tracy and her team knew there were a few departments that were not receptive to the coaching and development they could provide. She offered their services to all departments but focused on working with the few groups that showed interest in, and would most benefit from, their support. At any time, the other groups could change their mind and receive help as well. Tracy recognized that the saying "You can lead a horse to water, but you can't make it drink" also applied to individual managers and teams. By not forcing her support onto the managers who were obviously not interested in working with her, Tracy was able to spend her time in a way that was more fruitful and satisfying.

Middle managers work hard to have a positive influence on as broad an audience as possible. When individuals or groups show that they are not receptive, focus your efforts and attention in another direction. This, of course, is not always possible. If a middle manager finds that the people who report directly to him or her are not receptive to management, then he or she needs to address and fix the problem. The manager cannot choose to manage another group instead. If, however, there are several possible projects to propose and work on, it is wise to consider which will receive more collaboration and cooperation when deciding how to manage your and your team's time and resources.

Technique 4: Overcommunicate, Be Inclusive, and Follow Up

Lou assumed that other managers understood his role and the functions of which he had ownership. It is rarely safe to assume that this kind of interdepartmental understanding exists. A better approach for Lou would have been to communicate more frequently and with a wider audience about the projects and initiatives that he and his group were undertaking. All middle managers should err on the side of overcommunication to reduce the likelihood of miscommunication, duplication of work, and contradictory information.

Technique 5: Analyze and Fix It

When Mike joined the company as controller, it was fraught with contradictory financial information and inaccurate reports. He rolled up his sleeves, dug into the numerical mess, and fixed many of the problems with the data. He also oversaw the creation of several reports that helped managers run their parts of the business more effectively. When faced with contradictory information, duplication of efforts, or miscommunication, great middle managers do whatever it takes to understand and solve the problem. Good analysis goes a long way toward reducing or eliminating these and other types of mucky-muck.

Technique 6: Ask Probing Questions to Reveal Motives and Hidden Agendas

Mindy was an intuitive manager who knew the right questions to ask to discover a person's real intent and motivation. At one meeting, a manager was recommending that they restructure several roles. Mindy asked several questions to determine this manager's motive for recommending the change. Privately, she speculated whether his agenda was to increase the size of his organization or if he thought the current department manager was doing a poor job. Mindy's open-ended questions helped to clarify the details of the manager's recommendation. High-impact middle managers know when and how to ask the right questions that help explain the intent and motivation behind others' comments and suggestions.

Technique 7: Repair Relationships

John and Barry knew that their relationship was dysfunctional, but it was not until they were honest with each other that they were able to repair the relationship and work together more effectively. Once they resolved the issues between them, both of their departments experienced less mucky-muck.

It can be uncomfortable and difficult, but it is important for you to repair damaged relationships with current employees or coworkers. When not dealt with, these poor relationships will get in the way of communication, work flow, and results. Repairing a relationship does not mean that you have to socialize with each other; it means being able to work together productively and collaboratively. Workplace relationships should facilitate rather than hinder productive work.

Technique 8: Believe in the Capacity People Have for Change and Learning

If Tim had not looked past his employees' learned helplessness, he might have written them off as poor performers. Instead, he created a work environment that nurtured creativity and initiative. It took a while, but most of the previously lethargic employees became more engaged and passionate about their work. They accepted the changes that Tim was implementing and offered ideas for additional improvements. Great middle managers know that most performance problems are actually management or system problems and that, given the right guidance and leadership, nearly all employees will have the desire and capacity to do a great job. Mucky-muck can get in the way of people doing their best work, but the damage does not have to be permanent.

Technique 9: Get Organized

When Sally started her new job, she took over for an extremely unorganized manager. The first couple of months were difficult for Sally, and she felt set up to fail. Mucky-muck that comes from disorganization is common but is also the easiest kind to fix. Once Sally created a filing system and a routine that worked for her, she gained control of her department and became productive and successful. High-impact middle managers know that they need to stay organized to ensure that they and their teams are efficient and feel confident about their work. Whether done daily, weekly, or as needed, creating and practicing methods for organizing work is an important skill for middle managers. (Chapters 7 and 9 offer several techniques for staying organized.)

Technique 10: Lighten Up and Roll with It

Tim was an intense middle manager who let mucky-muck frustrate him. He asked why it was that things had to be a certain way or why it wasn't easier to get work done. This emotional reaction got in the way of his moving past the mucky-muck and getting his job done. It would have been better for him to shrug his shoulders, chuckle a bit, and rethink how to get the work done. Like Tim, some middle managers take mucky-muck too seriously. They get upset about the inefficiencies and frustration mucky-muck causes, which keeps them from being able to navigate through the mucky-muck. When dealing with mucky-muck, the first action you can take is to see it for the ridiculous barrier that it is. The middle managers who prevail despite it all are able to quickly move beyond the barriers. They know there are many ways to make a difference, and that they can do great work even when faced with mucky-muck. Sometimes, the best approach is just to laugh at it and move on.

Technique 11: See and Enjoy Accomplishments

Jim was grumbling to Lou about how hard it was to work in their organization because of all the mucky-muck he faced daily. Lou agreed but chose to see it another way. Although Jim was right about the mucky-muck, Lou saw the situation as inspiring and hopeful. They had a great middle management team that accomplished much under difficult working conditions.

They had been successful in creating major change and improvements within a work environment that was rife with politics, disorganization, and other permeations of mucky-muck. What an accomplishment!

Moreover, they were learning skills that would benefit their careers and enable them to prevail in almost any work environment. Yes, it was frustrating, and, yes, getting things done should not have been so hard, but the success of the team was worthy of celebration. Middle managers who produce results and get through the mucky-muck should recognize and take pride in the work they do and the results they achieve against the odds.

Summing Up

High-impact middle managers practice these 11 techniques to reduce and eliminate mucky-muck from their work environment. They try to bring perspective to each challenge and strengthen weak communication channels that are often at the core of mucky-muck. These techniques are also excellent methods for managing other complex or emotionally charged situations. Once you practice seeing and managing mucky-muck, you will become skilled at recognizing emerging problems and preventing them from undermining morale and derailing projects.

Be Part of the Solution, Not the Problem

As a high-impact middle manager, you need to be careful that you do not become a mucky-muck generator. Now that it is clear what mucky-muck is and how it damages productivity and results, you have the responsibility to own the mucky-muck that you create and to eliminate it. There are significant benefits in doing so. First, your work will be more meaningful and successful when not deluged with self-inflicted mucky-muck. Second, middle managers who ensure that they do not become part of the problem will enjoy others' respect and trust. To make your workplace productive, use these guidelines:

- Plan and communicate work plans in clear and complete terms.
- Communicate openly and candidly with managers, peers, and employees.

- Understand the motivations and intentions behind your ideas and suggestions. Share them honestly.
- Share projects and initiatives with peers at the formative stage of planning and implementation.
- Be a good corporate citizen. Represent the company and management well.
- Support employees so they can fully take on and own the work appropriate to their job.

On the other hand, do not do the following:

- Gossip or bad-mouth others.
- Obstruct or otherwise subtly sabotage changes.
- Allow differences in style or personality to get in the way of working productively with a peer or employee.
- Interfere with or take over a project or task that one of your employees owns.
- Let work pile up or become disorganized.
- Play favorites or make business decisions based on friendship.

By following these guidelines, you can have an immediate and positive impact on your work environment. Mucky-muck can be full of uncomfortable emotions, and dealing with them is draining. Reducing mucky-muck frees up mental and physical energy that can be used to do great work. Start calling the barriers you face mucky-muck in the presence of others and notice how referring to them in this silly way can help reduce their power and importance.

Chapter 7

....

Organizational Alignment: Ensuring That the Department Delivers Results

Awell-aligned department hums with efficiency. Processes for getting the work done are clearly understood and effective. Staff members' roles support the goals of both their work team and the company. Individuals are clear about what they should contribute. They are appropriately empowered and expect to produce results. Communication to and from departments facilitates each team's ability to remain on course and prioritize. The organizational structure and individual roles enable team members to identify and solve problems quickly. Work is more satisfying because it makes sense.

In contrast, poorly aligned organizational structures and processes cause numerous problems with quality, throughput, and results. When a structure or process is out of alignment with the larger goal it was designed to support, it no longer serves the goals of the team and company. Poor alignment can occur for various reasons. Perhaps changes have occurred in one area of the organization but not in others. Sometimes the problem is a lack of effective processes for getting the work done. Or it could be that roles have changed but processes have not, or visa versa.

A common reason for poor alignment is conflict among technology, processes, and roles. For team members, a poorly aligned organization feels disorganized, and getting work done seems more difficult than it should. Ambiguous, confusing, and overlapping roles are also signs of poor alignment. The design and planning of work flow is significant and should be a major focus for middle managers. Many middle managers, however, assume that unproductive people are to blame for poor results. Though there may be personnel problems for the manager to resolve, it is more likely that the department's processes and structures are responsible for the poor results.

Elements of Organizational Structure

The organizational structure defines job roles, departmental interdependencies, and communication channels. Structure determines who makes the decisions, and the depth and breadth of each person's role. Structure assigns responsibilities and accountabilities. The high-impact middle management definition of a middle manager is someone who oversees and is responsible for at least one structure and/or function that exists within the larger company's structure. For example, a middle manager who leads the sales and marketing departments may oversee a sales organization structure, a marketing structure, and one or more cross-functional project teams, each with their own structure. The human resources director may oversee one large structure that encompasses the entire department, with several smaller structures supporting the functions of recruiting, benefits, and training.

Processes are ways of working within a structure. They may be as elaborate and complicated as a computer-controlled manufacturing line or as simple as a way to deliver mail throughout an office. There are also de facto processes, or processes that have evolved and become standard practice without intentional design or planning. Most middle managers oversee several processes. Inefficient or irrelevant processes hurt results and cause productivity to suffer. This chapter will help middle managers ensure that they have the right structure and processes in place to produce results.

As a high-impact middle manager, you should continuously evaluate and realign structures and processes. Doing so will give you and your team the best chance for success. When results are inadequate, ask yourself, your team members, and your peers if the way the work is being done is enabling results or getting in the way of them. Are the processes and procedures that have been established setting you up for success or failure?

Best Practices for Organizational Alignment

High-impact middle management organizational alignment is a set of practices that enables middle managers to keep their structures and processes relevant and productive. These practices begin by looking at your department, and the work it produces, from a 50,000-foot-high view, or broad perspective, to answer one fundamental question: Is this department set up for success? High-impact middle managers regularly look at their functions in this way because they know that keeping roles and processes aligned is critical to ensuring optimal throughput and results. Once the big picture is clear, you can begin to focus on aspects of the structures and processes that need attention to deliver results. Organizational alignment should follow these best practices:

- Clarify the vision, purpose, and goals of the department.
- Use clean slate creativity to design an ideal organization model.
- Compare the needs of the department, the ideal organizational model, and current roles and processes.
- Generate alternatives that improve the organization.
- Realign structure, processes, roles, and procedures for maximum efficiency.
- Measure and monitor processes and work flow.

High-impact middle management organizational alignment will help you ensure that your work structures and processes mesh in a way that enables team members to be their most productive and deliver results. Let's look at each of the six best practices.

Practice 1: Clarify the Department's Vision, Purpose, and Goals

The middle manager, his or her manager, and the team members should all agree on the vision of the department's success and the expectations the company has for the department (see chapter 5). These expectations should represent and reflect the needs and wants of both internal and external customers. The sidebar gives an example of what the vision, purpose, and goals might look like for an organization's accounting department.

The accounting department is an internal service group and has an opportunity and responsibility to provide responsive and helpful service to both internal and external customers. This includes providing accurate and timely information, proactive analysis, resolution of problems, and responses to questions. There is also an expectation that, as the accounting experts, the department's staff will ensure that the company is following proper procedures to ensure fiscal accuracy and compliance with important regulations and audit principles. As the company expands its presence on the Internet, it is expecting the accounting function to support and reconcile business transactions produced via the web. Over the next year, the accounting team's major goals are to

- Improve the efficiency of invoice processing to reduce errors by 50 percent and improve processing speed by 15 percent, while at the same time maintaining or reducing current processing costs.
- Improve purchasing and payment processes related to field operations so that communications and information exchange are more efficient and the cost of the processing is reduced by 10 percent or more.
- Design and launch accurate and helpful reports that enable department managers to manage their areas more proactively and effectively. This effort should lead to an overall reduction in budget variances by the third month of implementation.
- Create and implement by June a strategy that supports the company's plans for selling products and services on its website. Develop online cash register services and reconciliation methods to ensure the proper collection and management of revenues.

A department's statement of its vision, purpose, and goals is an important tool for middle managers. It should become part of the department's playbook (see chapter 5) and be posted for employees, peers, and managers to see. When you take the time, as a middle manager, to crystallize and clarify your department's vision, purpose, and goals, you build a foundation for creating organizational alignment.

Practice 2: Use Clean Slate Creativity to Design an Ideal Organization Model

To realign structures and processes, it is important to start the design process with a clean slate before considering current resources, processes, and roles. Using clean slate creativity means designing, from the ground up, the ideal way a team and its processes should function to produce the vision and goals (see the sidebar for more details). For this exercise, do not think about current personnel, roles, resources, or processes. Instead, you should define how the work would be designed if nothing were already in place—hence the clean slate metaphor. These questions will help get your creative juices flowing:

- What is the long-term direction of the company, and how should the manager and team design today's work with this in mind?
- What is the most important work this team could do?
- What needs to be accomplished to meet or exceed the team's goals? Look at each goal individually, then look at the goals as a whole.
- To do this work, what roles are required? How should the department divide work among individuals and teams?
- How should managers and team members make decisions?
- What should the key processes be, and how should they work? What processes would make the work easier and more efficient?
- What role should technology play?
- How would the team and processes link to the rest of the company?
- What are the advantages and disadvantages of this organizational design?
- What human, process, and technological resources are needed to make this organizational structure work?
- If there were no limitations on resources, how would you and your team design the department's structure?

If it is feasible, you may find it helpful to have the entire team contribute to creating this design. The product of this creative work is an ideal view of what the organization and work processes would look like if designed from scratch to produce the department's vision, purpose, and goals. In addition to the clarifying roles, it is important to identify the processes that would make the team's work easier and more efficient. Depending on the scope and breadth of the work you are assessing, this exercise could take several hours or even days.

Clean Slate Creativity versus Problem Solving

There are two distinct ways you, as a middle manager, can approach a situation that needs improvement. You can choose clean slate creativity or employ a problem-solving approach. In using the clean slate approach, define how you would manage the work if there were no processes currently in place and no limitations on resources. To be successful using this method, do not to let your ideas become bogged down or hampered by current processes, people, or corporate culture. You can recognize current resources and limitations later in the redesign process.

When using a problem-solving approach, begin with today's roles, processes, and circumstances, and then define ways to improve results or performance from this current reality. Ideas conceived using this approach will more likely be similar and complementary to the work and processes your department is already using. Thus, the problem-solving approach works best when your department only needs to make minor changes or adjustments, not redesign an organization or process. Ideas that come from clean slate creativity will be more innovative, more creative, and more likely to lead to significant improvements in productivity.

Middle managers should complete this clean slate creativity exercise for their entire department at least once every two years, and then follow up with smaller redesign efforts for specific areas as needed. For example, if your company launches a new product line, a portion of the department's work and processes may need realignment. If there is one available, having a facilitator guide you and your team through these conversations is often helpful and allows a middle manager to participate fully.

Practice 3: Compare Department Needs, the Ideal Plan, and Current Roles and Processes

Once the ideal organizational design is complete, middle managers will be ready to bring the current reality into the realignment process and conversation. It is important to include a discussion of de facto processes—meaning those processes that you and your and team have not purposefully designed or implemented but that have developed over time. There are generally many more processes in place than middle managers recognize. For example, communication and problem resolution are areas where de facto processes are common.

During this part of the realignment, you will need to blend the ideal scenario with current roles, personnel, and processes. There is always going to need to be some give and take and some compromises. It is important to stand firm and resolute for the changes that are most important and be flexible and nimble in areas where multiple approaches might work. You and your team should answer these questions:

- How far apart are the ideal organizational model and the current organization? What are the differences and similarities?
- Is the ideal organization possible and practical?
- If the ideal organization is worth attaining, what might a transitional organization look like? How can the department begin its journey to ideal alignment?
- What aspects of the current organization and processes should not be changed? (Challenge the thinking behind the answers to these questions.) Why should these processes or roles stay the same?
- What further information or research do you and your team need to understand these ideas and choices? (Do this analysis and research before making decisions.)
- What objections or concerns will senior managers or peers have about these ideas? Are they valid? How can you and your team overcome these objections?

Again, using a facilitator to guide you and your team through this process is helpful and advised. A facilitator can see where the team is getting bogged down and where its thinking might need to be challenged. If a facilitator is not available, you will need to do a thorough job of planning the agenda and discussion questions before the meeting. After this conversation, you will know the ideas that have been placed on the table and the pros and cons of each. You will also have a good idea of how much needs to change to create alignment. This is a useful and illuminating process.

A word about team member participation: The general rule is that you should include input from team members and peers as much as possible. Depending on the nature of the realignment, it may not be appropriate to include team members in discussions about redesigning roles and processes. If jobs might be eliminated, then team members should not participate in the final design of roles. If team members ask whether jobs might be cut (they are probably wondering, even if they do not ask), it is best to be open and honest. You can say that the purpose of the organizational realignment and redesign is to figure out how the department can be more efficient and effective. This may mean that some processes and jobs will change or be affected, but the final details will not be clear until the realignment plan is complete and approved. If people are likely to be affected, middle managers should get through the redesign process as quickly as possible. If the organizational realignment is going to be significant and include major role changes, it might be best to complete the entire redesign process confidentially and without team member participation. Middle managers who do not include team members in the redesign process should take extra care and caution to ensure that they are getting thorough and accurate information with which to make decisions.

Practice 4: Generate Alternatives for Organizational Improvement

As a middle manager, you should create two or three realignment approaches based on the information collected and the discussion that has occurred. If there is one alternative that seems significantly better than the other possible plans, then present only one plan. Because there is often more than one workable scenario, it is generally best to prepare and present more than one option. As the planning progresses, you may eliminate choices based on several criteria including cost, ease of use, technology, and mucky-muck. The exception to this rule is when the middle manager and team feel confident and positive about an organizational design they have created. If you have done your homework and included the appropriate people in discussions, then present this recommendation and sell it to the key stakeholders and decision makers. Energy and passion account for much of the success of any plan. Whether presenting one or more alternatives, each plan should include

- a review of the vision, purpose, and goals the realignment seeks to support
- the major reasons the realignment is necessary
- a review of the proposed realigned organization and processes, and the results that the proposed organization will produce
- transition plans for personnel roles and processes that would change
- a description of roles and interdependencies between team members
- a description of major processes
- an explanation of how the work will flow from and to other groups
- a breakdown of costs, including short-term and long-term cost effects.

Depending on the scope of the plan, preparing it could take anywhere from a few hours to a couple of weeks. For a narrow focus area or single process, the entire realignment can take less than a day. Don't rush the process if more analysis and creativity will make the plan significantly richer or better. As the plan is coming together, middle managers should play the devil's advocate and encourage team members to challenge it to ensure that it answers potential objections and meets the needs of supporters and potential naysayers. Present the options to several trusted peers and ask for their input. Adjust the plan as appropriate.

Present the plan and gain approval! Provide backup information and details as needed. Have this information ready and available when others ask questions. Take the time to prepare for the presentation of the plan, because this will speed up its approval. Be open to adjusting the plan to get full support.

Practice 5: Realign Structure, Processes, Roles, and Procedures

The implementation of new structures and processes is critical to the success of the realignment. To ensure that team members and peers support the new way of doing the work, middle managers should

- Work with management and human resources on the timing of the plan's implementation, especially if any individual jobs or positions are affected.
- Communicate the vision, the realignment plan, the transition plan, and the role of each team member. Discuss the plan with peers and gain their support. If an individual's job is changing significantly, talk with him or her one-to-one before making any team announcements.
- Create a project plan for the transition of roles and processes. Ensure that all team members and affected peers have a current copy of the plan. Hold daily or weekly progress chats as needed.
- Be sincerely open and ready to listen to any concerns, suggestions, or questions. Be flexible enough to accept that the plan may need to be altered. Take time every day to check in with team members and peers. Do not micromanage the process, but show support and invite feedback.

Practice 6: Measure and Monitor Processes and the Work Flow

As the realignment rolls out and takes hold, it is important to monitor and measure performance and productivity. After all, increased efficiency and effectiveness are why changes were made in the first place! Figures should be communicated clearly and discussed often. As well as being part of the departmental playbook, key figures and milestones should be posted in a visible place in the department. If team members are located in the field, you can send figures and results to each team member and discuss them during regular email and telephone conversations.

Ensuring that your department is set up for success is important work for middle managers. Team members are more productive and satisfied when roles and processes facilitate results. In an aligned organization, mucky-muck goes down and the work environment is more intrinsically motivating.

An aligned organization runs like a well-oiled machine. High-impact middle managers know that to ensure their teams are set up for success, processes and roles need to be evaluated regularly as changes occur. When processes are inefficient, they produce waste and cause team members to work harder to get results. When roles are unclear or do not encompass new expectations, team members cannot do their best work. The high-impact middle management organizational alignment will help middle managers get results efficiently.

Chapter 8

High-Impact Leaders Are Unstoppable! Wiping Out Limitations to Results

Marty was talented and creative—a great catch for the company. He was hired to take over the leadership of an internal service department that was not meeting its deadlines and producing low-quality work. He had the right vision and understood the importance of delivering high-quality work that was on time and on budget. Thus, his managers were puzzled when the timeliness of the department's work went from bad to worse under his management.

To ensure that the planning, timeliness, and quality of the work was acceptable, Marty oversaw and reviewed all the work his group produced. Everything flowed through him and relied on his stamp of approval. Because quality was an issue and he wanted to develop his team's ability to recognize and solve problems, he reworked many of the projects himself. The quality of the work improved, but the completion rate was getting worse because he micromanaged every project. He also needed to spend time evaluating vendors and creating a long-term strategic plan for the department. There was not enough Marty to go around, and his involvement in projects had become a constraint.

Paul, another manager in Marty's organization, felt stuck. He needed to create and implement a plan to upgrade his team's skills and professionalism, but he put off the work again and again. He turned down help when it was offered. Time slipped away, and he did not have his plan ready or implemented in time for the next hiring season. He didn't know how to plan well. He had a tendency to be reactive instead of proactive, and he was often uncoachable when the topic of planning or time management came up. He often let the needs of the day divert his attention, and he never got around to completing the plan.

Corky knew she needed to get candidates through the selection and hiring process more quickly and efficiently, but she was at a loss about where to start. The selection and hiring process had many parts, each a potential place for breakdowns and delays. The application flow was good, but sometimes the applications sat for a while before anyone had time to review them. At times, interviews took longer than expected because of schedule conflicts. Reference checks, background checks, and drug screenings took more time than Corky preferred, but these processes relied on outside vendors who would not commit to faster results. The best candidates also needed to give their current employer two weeks' notice before leaving. Corky wondered what changes she could make that would optimize the hiring process while taking into account the resources available to her.

Maximizing Throughput

Marty, Paul, and Corky struggled with challenges that limited their results. Maximizing throughput to deliver products and services is an important responsibility of all middle managers. Throughput is the rate at which a person, department, system, or function produces results. Throughput may be expressed in terms of speed, quantity, time, or a combination of these factors. Most work can be described in terms of throughput. The time it takes to make decisions is throughput. The number of completed calls may be throughput. The accuracy of completed payroll check runs is throughput. Manager capacity can even be thought of in terms of throughput.

Middle managers are in the best position to recognize and resolve problems that limit throughput because they see and interact with many levels and layers of work, systems, and processes. In addition, it makes sense for middle managers to be concerned with and interested in throughput, because throughput leads to results. Middle managers are often the most directly accountable for producing results. Focusing on and improving throughput may come naturally to some middle managers; those who come from a traditional manufacturing or product distribution background are most likely to have had experience in this area. Many middle managers, however, have had neither training nor experience in solving throughput problems.

A disciplined and focused day-to-day management practice is essential to understanding and improving throughput. Once major problems are resolved, middle managers should still be prepared to monitor and troubleshoot throughput on a regular basis. Factors that limit throughput may change daily or be a continuing problem. In either case, middle managers who are prepared to quickly identify and deal with these problems get better results. Middle managers must seek out and remove barriers to throughput, using analysis, conversation, observation, and interactive "management by walking around."

What Reduces Throughput?

Several common business practices and actions can limit throughput. Sometimes, making one change can improve throughput; while at other times, combining several actions will work best. You should also be cautious about making changes. For example, making a change in one area may cause problems in other areas. There are several ways to look at throughput, and each offers a unique view of potential problems and limiting factors. No one approach is likely to be appropriate all the time. The most important skill for middle managers is to be able to recognize what is getting in the way of results. Learning this skill can sometimes be a challenge and may require that a middle manager use more than one "model," or way of looking at how the work gets done. Let's look at the eleven most common types of problems affecting throughput and a sampling of approaches used for solving them.

Problem 1: Bottlenecks

A bottleneck is a point of congestion that reduces the flow of work and hinders progress and productivity. One way to recognize a bottleneck is by the work that piles up before the bottleneck and the people or process steps that are waiting for work coming from the bottleneck. There may be more than one bottleneck in a workflow or process. Figure 8-1 shows a simple process. Steps B and C are bottlenecks because they cannot process as much work as can steps A and D. If step A consistently pushes at a rate of 25 per day and step B at a rate of 20, work will pile up before steps B and C; and step D will sometimes be idle, or pulling on step C for more work.

Figure 8-1. A Simple Process with Two Bottlenecks

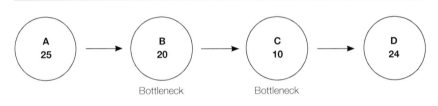

Figure 8-2 shows another common situation that produces bottlenecks. In this example, three separate processes all use the same resource, step C/L/S. A resource can be a person, a process step, a piece of machinery, or a computer function. This resource can handle the workload of any one process, but not all three. Step C/L/S is a major bottleneck. Steps J, K, B, and Q are also bottlenecks.

The story about Marty at the beginning of this chapter was an example of a bottleneck created when a resource serves multiple processes. Marty supported all processes in his department; but as a single resource, he could not keep up with the demands from upstream and downstream customers and suppliers.

Problem 2: Constraints

A constraint is the bottleneck that has the most impact on overall throughput and results. There is only one constraint in a process or system (unless there are two bottlenecks that have the same throughput rate). In fact, one constraint may affect several processes. A constraint can be a person, system, process step, piece of machinery, or computer function. In the previous example, Marty is both a bottleneck and a constraint.

Figure 8-2. Three Processes with a Common Bottleneck

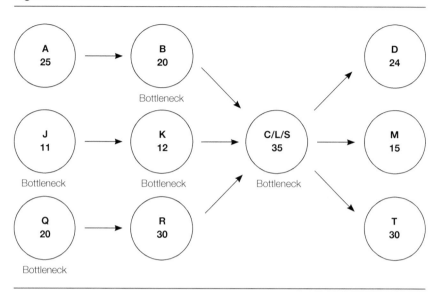

Figure 8-3 shows a simple process with both the bottlenecks and the constraint identified. Step C is the constraint because it has the most impact on output. This process has a throughput of 10, because that is the capacity of the constraint. Remember the saying "A chain is only as strong as its weakest link"? The same logic holds true for throughput. The process step with the lowest capacity sets the pace of throughput. It is not always easy to find the constraint.

In figure 8-3, the answer is simple. Looking at figure 8-2 again, it is not clear which step is the constraint. To decide this, the manager will

Figure 8-3. A Bottleneck and Constraint

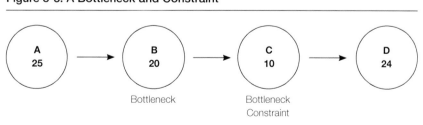

need to calculate the time the C/L/S resource spends on each process vying for its time. If C = 10, L = 10, and S = 15, then this resource is the constraint for all three processes. If C = 23, L = 12, and S = 0, the C/L/S resource would be the constraint for the Q/R/S/T process (in fact, this process has stalled) but not for the other two processes. In this case, step B and step J are the constraints for the other two processes. If Marty is the C/L/S resource, it would help to identify how he spends his time and how his choices are affecting each project or process that relies on him. It is common for middle managers to spread their time evenly and become a bottleneck or constraint in many work processes or to focus on one or two projects and become the constraint on others. Neither of these approaches maximizes throughput.

Problem 3: Slow Process Connections

Sometimes the connections between resources affect throughput more than the steps of the process itself. This is particularly a problem with work processes that rely on two or more handoffs between people in the same or different departments. Figure 8-4 shows a three-step process with two handoffs.

The process steps to make a purchase add up to a total time of three to four days. However, the total order-processing time is much longer, as much as 8 to 11 days, or up to almost three times longer! Process connections can often account for as much as or more than the total throughput time spent in the process steps. It is common for work to sit and wait

Figure 8-4. A Three-Step Process with Two Handoffs

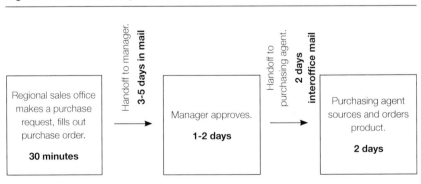

for the next person or process step to move it forward. Much of the time spent between process steps is wasted and is a common cause of reduced throughput. Processes with many steps are particularly vulnerable to the effects of slow process connections. It is important to define the time used by process connections and process steps, because the methods for improving throughput are different depending on where the inefficiencies lie.

Problem 4: Lengthy or Complicated Critical Paths

A critical path shows the minimum amount of time a process or project will take to be completed by identifying interdependent steps. Dependencies among steps slow processes. For example, if new computers cannot be purchased until the capital budget is approved, then the work on installing new computers is dependent on the budget approval; and this has to be taken into account when determining the time it will take to complete the project. Some work can occur concurrently, while other work depends on the completion of a previous step. A critical path shows middle managers which interdependencies are affecting the overall throughput rate.

Figure 8-5 shows a simple critical path. In this example, the minimum critical path is six weeks and four days long. In other words, if everything goes well, and assuming the process connections are efficient,

Figure 8-5. A Simple Critical Path

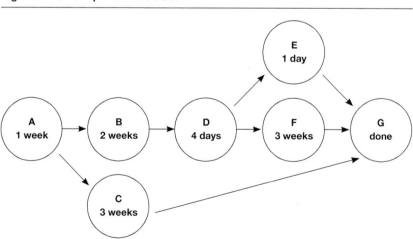

the work will take no less than six weeks and four days. Steps A, B, D, and F are on the critical path. They set the pace of results because of their dependency on one another. Step B cannot begin until step A is complete. Step F cannot begin until step D is complete, but it can begin concurrently with step E. Step C can begin after step A, but then it does not affect other steps.

Remember Corky from earlier in the chapter? She needed to improve the speed and efficiency of the hiring process. It is likely that the process suffered from a long critical path and that she would have to change this to make any real improvements to hiring throughput. Figure 8-6 illustrates what her hiring process looked like.

The critical path for the hiring process is a minimum of 24 days long! This assumes there is a steady stream of applications and that the recruiter does not need to advertise the position. If there are not enough applicants, the hiring process is 30 to 35 days long. Given that most employees only provide two weeks' notice before leaving the company, it is difficult for Corky's team to meet the organization's needs. The critical path for her hiring process is too long and does not serve her goal of having new employees in place when needed.

Problem 5: Skills Deficiencies

One of the more common reasons for slower throughput of general work assignments and projects is a middle manager's inability to plan, monitor, and assign work. When middle managers have not learned the skills needed to organize and prioritize work, they put off the wrong tasks and waste time fighting preventable fires.

Paul did not plan well, and this got in the way of his success. He worked hard and cared about the quality and success of his team. What he could not see was that his inability to make better time management choices hurt his department and his career. He had a long to-do list, but he failed to realize that all his tasks were not equal. He did not have the experience or know-how to recognize important critical paths. To start the new season off well, he needed to be planning and making several important decisions six months in advance.

Figure 8-6. Corky's Hiring Process

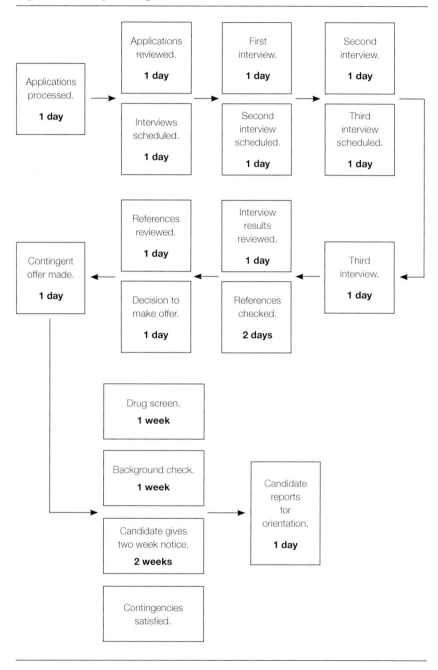

Instead, Paul spent his time on what was most pressing in his mind, which was work on a project due in a month. That work was important, too, but he could have delegated it or delayed working on it for a week or two. He needed to create the departmental plan; however, by the time he got around to thinking about it, several important deadlines had passed. Inexperienced middle managers, like Paul, often do not feel the sense of urgency when it comes to planning and do not understand that the lead time needed for planning is just as important a deadline as those for other pressing tasks. Middle managers need to be excellent planners and communicators to ensure that the work keeps flowing.

Other skills shortages also get in the way of throughput. Middle managers who have not developed their abilities to partner, manage performance, set goals, or coach others will also suffer from lower throughput. Other chapters of this book address these skills.

Problem 6: Breakdowns

Breakdowns are system or process failures. People can also be the cause of breakdowns. Personal illnesses, vacations, and other situations that cause a person to stop working on a task could be considered breakdowns. When Tim first looked at the throughput in his department, he found that an excessive use of sick days by several of his staff members caused lower productivity and work quality.

Problem 7: Errors

Errors are mistakes that cause work to have to be reworked or lead to other additional work. The accounting department spent an average of six person-hours per week fixing accounts payable check run errors, or 5 percent of the team's total human resources! With a group of just three employees, this represents a significant waste of resources, which had a negative impact on their throughput.

Problem 8: Waste

Waste, as it relates to throughput, is work that is substandard or not usable—or work that, though satisfactory, is not used. When an employee copies and then distributes reports that few read, this is waste. The reports are usable, but few people are using them. It is also considered waste when marketing materials are scrapped due to inaccurate information. Waste uses resources that could otherwise be used for work that makes a difference. Waste reduces throughput potential. Reducing waste can be an easy and effective way to boost throughput without adding cost or resources.

Problem 9: Changes

Changes affect throughput in a variety of ways. When changes occur, error rates and waste may also increase. In addition, many changes result in temporary skills deficiencies and work pace slowdowns. Middle managers should take into account the potential impact that changes will have on throughput. Though some temporary productivity dips may be acceptable, a good middle manager should have some strategies in place for minimizing disruption.

Problem 10: Employee Turnover

Employee turnover results in skills deficiencies, higher error rates, slower work paces, breakdowns, and waste. Throughput is often disrupted when employees leave.

Problem 11: Inadequate Worker Training

When changes and improvements are made, workers need to be retrained. Some skills are specialized enough so that refresher training will improve throughput. When workers do not have the right training, they cannot do their best work.

Summing Up

Is it any wonder that a middle manager's job is so tough? Many things affect throughput. One of your most challenging and important responsibilities as a middle manager is to do whatever is necessary to diagnose and solve these problems to improve results. However, deciding what action will make the most difference is not always easy or straightforward.

Becoming Unstoppable: Techniques for Improving Throughput

High-impact middle managers know how to zero in on problems affecting throughput. They focus on the areas posing the most significant challenges and systematically remove them or lessen their effect. Sometimes the toughest part is determining what the problem is. These techniques facilitate maximizing throughput and results when practiced regularly:

- establishing a results-oriented environment
- diagnosing throughput problems
- solving throughput problems
- asking the right questions.

Establishing a Results-Oriented Environment

Middle managers who create work environments in which their employees quickly identify, openly discuss, and creatively solve problems will outproduce managers who do not. Managers cannot realistically expect to discover and tackle each problem themselves. When teams work together to ensure that nothing gets in the way of throughput, work is more productive and satisfying. Managers will know when this environment exists because improvements and problem solving happen naturally.

To create a results-oriented environment, middle managers should react positively and supportively to employees who bring problems to their attention. Do your employees feel comfortable discussing problems or errors? Do they feel sure that you care and want to know about the good, the bad, and the ugly? Do you provide negative reinforcement for raising questions or challenging ideas? Do your employees feel appreciated for their efforts to solve problems?

Case Study

Harry's employees did not share their ideas with him very often. His first and most natural response was to be defensive. Even when his staff was not laying blame in his direction, it seemed as though he took most any concern, criticism, or alternative idea as a personal censure. He also had a tendency to want to cover up problems in his area. Once, he had several managers who were bottlenecks to an important change the company was making. Instead of being open about this problem, he led senior management to believe that these managers backed the change effort and that there would be no problems with the implementation. When the senior managers later found out about the resistance, he said that he didn't know it existed—even though his staff had told him about it weeks earlier. He gave his managers no reason to be proactive in identifying and communicating problems or barriers. As a result, they were reactive, and their throughput suffered.

Middle managers who want to create a results-oriented work environment should be sure that they are accessible and responsive. Having regular and informal conversations with team members provides an opportunity for sharing news about the work. Managers who ask open-ended questions rooted in curiosity and support (versus those rooted in control) will discover people's concerns and ideas. Practicing management by walking around daily helps middle managers stay in tune with daily happenings. These social activities serve a practical purpose. Managers who know what is going on in their department can better react to areas that need their time and support. Managers who routinely close their office doors or are inaccessible are not using communication—one of the most valuable management tools to improve throughput.

Diagnosing Throughput Problems

There are many possible reactions to barriers or problems affecting throughput. Deciding which actions will provide the greatest benefit requires analysis and diagnosis. The 80/20 rule applies here. One or a few remedies (20 percent) will have a more significant impact (80 percent) on results than most other possible actions. Your goal is to determine which responses will have the maximum benefit. To do this, it is important to classify the type of limitations getting in the way of throughput. The following questions can help you decide how to focus their improvement efforts. Ask them with a process, system, or project in mind that is not experiencing satisfactory throughput:

- Is this process, system, or project plagued by bottlenecks?
- Is there more than one identifiable bottleneck?
- Is there a step, person, or part of the process that is holding up progress and forward movement of the work?
- Can you identify the constraint or the pacesetter?
- Is there a large difference between how long the work takes at each step and the total time of completion?
- Do handoffs between process or project steps take longer than wanted?
- Is the critical path too long?
- Are there opportunities to look at reducing dependencies between steps or tasks?
- Is the manager struggling to stay on top of the demands on his or her time?
- Does the manager lack practical experience or training in how to plan and communicate work?
- Is mucky-muck a major problem impacting productivity?
- Have there been any breakdowns or shutdowns that have affected this work?
- Is this process, project, or system plagued by errors?
- Does this process, system, or project waste time, energy, or resources?
- Has change had a negative impact on the work?
- Has the team working on this process, project, or system suffered from the turnover of personnel?
- Do any team members lack the skills to keep the work flowing?

For those questions to which the answers are unknown, take a moment to analyze and discover the answer. You may find that creating a worksheet with these questions and answers will help you to further clarify the issues. Taking the time to draw a diagram of the process or work flow can be enlightening as well. Middle managers can draw almost any work process or project using circles and arrows, as pictured in the figures earlier in this chapter. Be sure to define each process connection, because these handoffs are often a source of waste. Notice where the bottlenecks are and the single step or person that is the constraint. What is the pace of the constraint? If the pace is acceptable, then bottlenecks and constraints are not your primary problem. Next, try to create the critical path. When first defining a critical path, it is often surprising how many steps a process contains and how long the critical path is.

Each "yes" response in the worksheet suggests a possible focus for improvement. Once completed, the worksheet will help you evaluate various possible opportunities to improve throughput. Specific techniques that address areas of opportunity follow. After reviewing these suggestions, you will be able to determine which improvements will have the highest impact on results.

Eli Goldratt's Theory of Constraints

The author, scientist, and educator Eliyahu Goldratt has advanced the science and practice of understanding throughput, constraints, and bottlenecks. In his books—*The Goal, It's Not Luck,* and *Critical Chain*—he shares his theory of constraints in a way that is helpful to middle managers who want to improve their results. Middle managers who oversee numerous or major processes or projects will benefit from reading his books and learning about his theory of constraints. This book does not seek to teach or explain the theory of constraints; rather, it is a general introduction for middle managers to various approaches to diagnosing and solving problems with throughput. You can find other resources on his website, www.toc-goldratt.com.

Solving Throughput Problems

Once a source for the throughput problem has been identified, middle managers should focus their improvement efforts on finding the solution that will most improve results. For the best results, and whenever possible, you should involve team members and peers in defining and implementing each solution. Involving others will improve commitment and accuracy, and will speed up the implementation of changes. Let's look at six of the most common types of solutions.

Solution 1: Distinguish Constraints from Bottlenecks

Middle managers may waste time removing bottlenecks that are not constraints. Individuals, teams, or departments who seek to optimize their part of a process without looking at the whole picture are most likely to face this problem. Here is a simple process with both the bottlenecks and the constraint identified.

In this process, steps B, C, D, and E are bottlenecks and step D is the constraint. Work will pile up waiting for steps B and C to be completed and a huge pileup will accumulate before step D. The people or machines doing step E will sit idle if not utilized in other processes or projects.

Until step D's performance improves, the overall process will produce at an approximate pace of 10. If this were a process contained within one team, it would be obvious that step D should be the starting point for improvement. But what if this process spanned several departments? In this case, you would need to work together to identify the constraint and concentrate on improving performance. This example is a simple one, but middle managers can look at and analyze any work process or project in the same way. Understanding both bottlenecks and the constraint will give you a better picture of the potential options for improving throughput. Using the process depicted in figure 8-7, for example, the following questions might come to mind:

- What actions will improve step D's performance?
- Is there another resource, person, system, or machine that can take over some of step D's workload?
- What can the other process steps do to make step D's job easier and more efficient?
- Can steps A, B, and E provide resources to another process to improve its throughput?
- What throughput pace is acceptable? How can the work flow be optimized to enable the team to produce consistently at this pace?

Middle managers who take the time to identify and understand bottlenecks and constraints will have a valuable tool for improving results. Focusing on constraint performance will ensure that time and resources have the highest benefit.

Figure 8-7. A Process with Four Bottlenecks and One Constraint

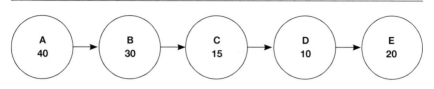

Solution 2: Reduce the Impact of Constraints

Once you identify a constraint, you can work to improve or supplement the constraint's performance. This is often the most valuable work that a middle manager can do, which makes this work a priority on the 80/20 list (the 20 percent of effort that produces 80 percent of the results). When dealing with constraints, consider using these steps:

1. *Test to ensure the proper identification of the constraint.* Constraints may be obvious or difficult to identify. To make sure that you identify the constraint correctly, ask yourself whether improving this process step would result in overall improvements to throughput. If the answer is yes, then it is more than likely that this resource is the constraint.

2. *Determine the potential capacity of the constraint.* The constraint capacity is the amount of work related to a particular process that can possibly be done under the best of circumstances. Middle managers need to be cautious not to consider a resource's total capacity when evaluating a constraint if the resource serves multiple processes or projects.

3. *Identify ways to improve capacity.* Is it always possible to improve the capacity of a resource? Sometimes yes, sometimes no. Simplification, automation, and upgrading abilities or skills are a few ways to improve the capacity of a resource.

4. *Identify additional resources to help lessen the constraint.* Sometimes a resource needs to be augmented to improve throughput. When the constraint is a person, you, as a middle manager, will want to look at delegating work away from the constraint and rebalancing the workload. When the constraint is a system step, augmenting performance means adding components or diverting work to another part of the process.

5. *Optimize the efficiency of the constraint through better setups and handoffs.* Middle managers may be able to improve the throughput of the constraint by changing the way work gets to and leaves this resource. If the process step preceding the constraint has excess capacity (relative to the pace of the constraint), then having it take extra time to better prepare the work going to the constraint will be time well spent. Can you or a team member more effectively organize, document, or communicate the work before it gets to the constraint? Can the upstream resource queue up the work more effectively? Is the slowest person or machine spending time doing work that people or machines before or after it can perform?

Solution 3: Reduce Bottlenecks When Necessary

In at least two situations, you as a middle manager will want to focus on reducing bottlenecks to throughput. First, you need to address bottlenecks that are likely to become the next constraint, especially if the current constraint is already a focus for improvement. Second, you will want to reduce bottlenecks as part of an overall process redesign or optimization. Improving bottleneck performance may allow it to augment the constraint's performance or become a resource for other processes. Here are some steps you can take:

1. *Test to ensure that improving this bottleneck will improve results.* Before you spend time and energy on improving the performance of a bottleneck, you should assess whether the effort will make enough of a difference to warrant investment. Will this improvement pass the 80/20 test?
2. *Determine the bottleneck's capacity.* How much high-quality work can this resource complete? Can this resource produce more?
3. *Identify ways to improve capacity.* Is the employee or process efficient? Are all elements of the work necessary? Is there an opportunity to automate or combine steps?
4. *Identify additional resources to decrease the effect of bottlenecks.* As they do when trying to improve constraint performance, middle managers should utilize other resources to help improve the overall performance of a process or project. Those who develop their skills in

workload balancing will find they have more choices for improving throughput.

5. *Optimize the efficiency of the bottleneck through better setups and handoffs.* It is important to ensure that work arrives at bottlenecks quickly and efficiently. If team members need to look up information or get an excessive number of approvals before beginning the work, their output will suffer. Bureaucracy and red tape often get in the way of progress, particularly when they affect a constraint or bottleneck.

Solution 4: Shorten Critical Paths

Many throughput problems occur because the process or project design does not support the needed pace of throughput. Middle managers often underestimate the time needed to get through the various parts of a process or critical path. Corky's hiring process was an example of this. She thought that candidates should be able to get through the hiring process in a week in addition to the two weeks' notice the candidate would need to give to his or her current employer—in other words, a total of 19 days. The critical path for the hiring process, however, took 24 days. Middle managers who take time to understand and improve the critical path of important work processes will be in a better position to improve their team's throughput and results. Here are some steps you can take when dealing with critical paths:

1. *Ensure that the critical path is accurate and complete; beware of hidden steps or delays!* When determining a critical path, managers should consider each component of the work, including smaller or shorter steps like approvals, paperwork, mailing times, and vendor lead times. It is also dangerous to assume the best-case scenario for estimating a critical path. Getting a signature on paperwork could happen in just a few minutes, but is this typical?

2. *Test assumptions about each step on the critical path.* If the critical path is unacceptably long, you, as a middle manager, can begin to shave time off by challenging the assumptions behind each step. Does the work need to take this long? Is every step necessary? Can process changes allow for more steps that are concurrent?

3. *Identify ways to shorten each step on the critical path.* Middle managers can make tasks more efficient by considering alternative ways of doing the work. Can team members transmit, communicate, and share information electronically? Which tasks are candidates for automation? Can team members reduce specific parts of the work and still produce high-quality results?

4. *Identify ways to shorten handoff times.* The critical path length may double when it includes the time needed for handoffs. The handoff, or process connection, often does not add any value to the work other than to facilitate communication and understanding. Reducing handoff times can be a quick and easy way to improve throughput. To reduce process connection delays, middle managers must first define them and objectively determine their length or time. Managers can then reduce the number of process connections by challenging the use of each handoff. Eliminate needless handoffs. For cross-functional processes, it may be necessary to collaborate with peers to diagnose the root causes of slow process connections to seek alternative approaches.

5. *Reduce unnecessary steps.* Most processes, particularly everyday work processes, have unnecessary steps. Identifying and eliminating unnecessary steps is the "low-hanging fruit" of process improvement. It is quick and effective, but it can only occur when middle managers analyze and evaluate work processes.

6. *Determine methods for doing more work concurrently, but ensure that doing so will improve throughput.* The more interdependent steps in the work process there are, the longer the critical path will be. To support an environment where team members can work on many tasks at the same time, middle managers must communicate the status and progress of the work often and fully.

Solution 5: Improve Skills

Training and development are useful managerial tools for improving throughput. Both you and your team members need to ensure that you have the skills needed to complete the work quickly and well. It can be difficult for middle managers to evaluate their own development needs, but it becomes easier when the focus is on results and throughput. Are you getting projects completed on time? Do you wish results were better? With what tasks do you struggle? Are you able to complete the analytical work needed to solve throughput problems? Are you able to plan well? The answers to these and other questions may help you determine new skills that could benefit your team:

1. *Objectively determine needed skills.* To maximize throughput, middle managers need to be excellent analyzers, planners, and communicators. The most common middle management development needs are in the areas of planning and organizing. These skills are also critical for improving throughput. Middle managers who struggle with deadlines and seem disorganized may need help and development in these areas. If your team members are unclear about their priorities and work assignments, then you definitely need training in planning and organizing. For team members, time management and problem identification are often skills that need improvement. Specific technical skills may also help the manager and his or her team members work more effectively.

2. *Identify teaching resources.* Who in the organization is strong in the area needing development? Can they mentor an employee needing development? What training options will work best in this case? Search for recent books, tapes, and articles on the topic. For middle managers who need to develop their ability to plan and analyze work, there are, unfortunately, fewer choices. Finding a mentor or coach within or outside the organization will probably be the best solution for developing these important skills.

3. *Establish learning follow-up and reinforcement.* Middle managers who take the time and energy to develop themselves and team members should also invest in follow-up and in reinforcing these newly developed skills. The best way to reinforce learning is to use the new skills! If team members have attended training, make sure they utilize the new skills they have learned. This will benefit the team and provide them with work that is likely to be intrinsically motivating.

Solution 6: Deal with Other Barriers to Throughput

Barriers to throughput regularly challenge middle managers. These general skills for diagnosing and solving problems will be invaluable tools for dealing with most of these challenges:

1. *Diagnose the root cause of problems affecting throughput.* Middle managers who ask why problems occur until they get to the root cause of an issue will be in a better position to effect real and lasting improvements. To diagnose the root causes of problems, excellent collaboration skills and a healthy sense of curiosity are important. Review each of the potential problems affecting throughput presented earlier in this chapter. Ask peers and team members for input. Test ideas and assumptions to determine if they are valid.

2. *Notice and address patterns, themes, and recurring barriers.* Many problems occur repeatedly but may go unnoticed for some time. Often, the only way to see and understand the problem is to take notice of and address patterns such as difficulty or recurring smaller issues. Is there a theme or pattern that could shed light on the underlying problem with a process or project?

3. *Become a barrier obliterator.* Middle managers who make it their mission to seek out and destroy barriers to throughput will improve results more quickly and completely than those who do not. Being proactive or reacting quickly is better than waiting until results deteriorate and the barriers no longer respond quickly to efforts at their removal. Middle managers lose precious time when they do not address emerging problems. High-impact middle managers often think about the things getting in the way of throughput and then they take action to improve results.

The Most Important Question Middle Managers Should Ask

Middle managers who want to improve throughput should always ask this question: "What are the one or two changes that will have the most impact on the overall throughput of this work?" Said another way, the question becomes "What is the 20 percent that will improve throughput by 80 percent?" Whether the focus is on the constraints, bottlenecks, critical paths, connections, skills, mucky-muck, or other barriers, the question is the same. A few improvements can have a significant and positive impact on results. Middle managers should seek out and implement these value-added improvements as much as possible.

It is not always easy to discern the changes that will have a significant impact from those that will not make much of a difference. To ensure that you have determined the best changes to make, ensure that adequate analysis and testing have been done. In addition, the impact previous changes have made should be assessed and considered. Do not make the same or similar mistakes repeatedly. Once your team implements a modification, they should closely monitor throughput to evaluate the effect the change is having.

Chapter 9

Using High-Impact Middle Management to Make the Most of Your Busy Day

Jim felt discouraged about how little he was accomplishing at work. Every day was an exercise in frustration, playing catch-up, and rolling tasks onto tomorrow's to-do list. He always felt behind the curve—despite working extra hours. He was not able to prioritize his schedule because everything seemed important; and he spent most of his day in meetings or talking with his managers. He knew that the ways in which he spent his time did not match up with his manager's priorities and expectations for him, but he still allowed himself to gravitate toward doing the work that was most comfortable for him, rather than what needed to get done. Though he talked a great deal about the importance of planning, he spent more time talking about planning than actually doing it. He used planners, to-do lists, and white boards, but still felt that he was not on top of things. In addition, he stalled out when he was emotionally uncomfortable with a task or decision.

Jim is not alone. Many middle managers have more tasks on their to-do list than they can ever complete, and they don't know what they can do to improve their situation. They wish they had a clone, or two, to help knock off more work. This state of affairs is endemic to the job of middle management and is not something that will go away by working two more hours each day. Working more is not the answer, and burnout the likely result. To gain control of their day, middle managers should examine how they are spending time and make choices that will yield better results.

Five Fallacies about Time

One of the barriers middle managers face regarding their time is their perception of time management. How many times have you heard yourself, or a fellow middle manager, utter these statements:

- Time is precious.
- There is never enough time!
- If it ain't broke, don't fix it.
- If it is worth doing, it's worth doing right.
- Slowing down decreases output.

All five of these statements are fallacies about time. If you are a busy middle manager who works too much (many middle managers fit into this group), the best solution to issues with time might be to change your beliefs about time and your definition of what successful use of your time looks like. Let's look at the five fallacies about time, which illustrate how beliefs can get in the way of good time management.

Fallacy 1: Time Is Precious

Most people—in their hearts and minds—believe that time is precious. That said, if someone were to follow you around all day, would that person get the sense that you valued time? For many managers, what they intend (to use time wisely) and what they do (give time away like it is a cheap commodity) are completely different.

Voni was a smart, hardworking middle manager who led the race and social justice program. Although she worked long days and on weekends, she felt that she was making good choices about how she spent her time. When pressed by her boss to take on another project, she pushed back, saying that she and her team did not have time. When he suggested that she do a time audit to see where her time was going, she realized that she had been wasting nearly a third of her day on activities that were not critical to her program's success.

All managers schedule their time with the best of intentions, but it is easy to let meeting invitations, off-topic drive-by conversations, and FYI (for your information) email exchanges suck time away from more important tasks.

Fallacy 2: There Is Never Enough Time!

As managers get older and retire, they rarely think back and wish they had spent more time at the office. If anything, their sentiments are quite the opposite. Many managers lament that they lost important parts of their lives by working too much. Time is a unit of life, a slice of one's experience here on Earth. A middle manager has more than 10,000 minutes each week to divvy up for what's most meaningful, important, or fun to do. Those who regularly choose to work too many hours a week are shortchanging other parts of their lives.

As a middle manager, making good choices about how to manage your time is not just a desirable thing to do, it is essential. Like a traffic cop in the middle of a busy intersection, middle managers need to make good decisions about which work moves forward and how quickly.

Managers who work more will often produce less. This may sound counterintuitive, but managers who routinely work late or on weekends are not as productive or effective as those who spend fewer hours at work. Although you may work more than 60 hours a week, your number of truly productive hours is generally less than 40. At a certain point, the exhaustion of working 60 hours a week will yield diminishing returns in terms of loss of concentration, diminished creativity, and low morale. The way to become more successful is not to work harder but to work smarter.

Mindy was a middle manager who worked too much. She was invited to take part in numerous meetings about all aspects of the agency, and people valued her input and ideas. She liked to participate, enjoyed knowing what was going on in the agency, and had a hard time saying no. Because these meetings took up so much of her day, she worked evenings and weekends to get her other work done. She allowed herself to become the go-to person for more topics than was practical or efficient. She accepted, and sometimes encouraged, scope creep, which broadened her job responsibilities to the point that she could do many things halfheartedly but only few well.

Deep down, Mindy knew this and was worried about it to the point that it took a toll on her health. When she was under pressure, she was jittery, had a nervous tic, and did not take the time to listen during conversations. She was present in body, but her mind was absent. This only exasperated the problem. She used her busy schedule as an excuse for not managing better. Senior management could see she was busy and working long hours, and, as a result, let her poor performance slide. Over time, her managers' expectations of her fell. Her job performance suffered, and she did not achieve the best results possible. Her life was out of balance.

Jane's work style was different but no more effective. In addition to spreading herself too thin and getting involved in too many tasks, she puttered her time away. She worked numerous hours, but many of them were spent on unimportant tasks. She did not know how to prioritize, plan, or execute work, and she did nothing to ensure that her team was working on the right action plans. As a result, she and her department spent their time on tasks that made little difference within the agency.

Jane allowed herself to spend several hours a day responding to routine requests and inquiries. A better use of her time would have been to build up the independence and capacity of her organization, so that each of her team members would be able to address and solve many of their daily issues. She focused on the tyranny of the urgent rather than on what was valuable. She also procrastinated until the last possible moment, and then she came in evenings and on weekends to get her work done on time, or at least not too late. However, she never left enough time, so her work was often poorly done and incomplete. She had more than enough time to get her job done, but she wasted most of it.

Jim, Mindy, and Jane would probably all say that if they only had more time, they could be more successful. The fact was that even if they had more time, their poor time management habits would get in the way, and they would end up producing the same unsatisfactory results. They did not need more time; they needed to spend their time more productively. Until middle managers are using their 40 hours a week optimally, they should resist the temptation to work more hours and throw the rest of their life out of balance.

Fallacy 3: If It Ain't Broke, Don't Fix It

One of the greatest wastes of time is continuing to do things the same way because it seems to be working. Often, middle managers do not even know if their processes, systems, or practices are serving the outcome, because they have not recently evaluated them. Sticking with the status quo may not save time and is more likely to waste it. What if there were a better way to do the work? Have the conditions that justified the current approach changed? What if the goals have changed but the work has not?

As the primary change agent within your agency, you, as a middle manager, need to question the status quo and ensure that processes and practices are set up to deliver the desired results. When goals change, practices and processes must also change. Hesitating or failing to change ideas or approaches that are comfortable wastes time and money. (Techniques for improving processes can be found in chapter 7.)

Jake told his middle managers that he wanted them to improve their analysis capabilities so they could make better decisions. The end goal was to increase productivity, quality, and profitability throughout the organization. It was a great strategy, but it proved hard to achieve. Jake and many of the other middle managers assumed that the goal of greater accountability and ownership could happen using their current agency practices. They were wrong.

As things stood, many of their agency's processes and systems did not support the type of functional analysis and optimization that Jake and the other managers wanted to implement. Middle managers could not get the data they needed to make sound judgments. In addition, team members did not buy into the idea that they should spend more time measuring their effectiveness, nor did they know how to accomplish this. Their comfortableness with the status quo was getting in the way and wasting time. To improve results, they needed to question whether their current processes and systems were satisfactory or needed to be changed.

Fallacy 4: If It Is Worth Doing, It's Worth Doing Right

The problem with this statement comes from how middle managers define "doing things right." If the standard for "right" is perfect or restrictive, then waiting to do things right could lead to procrastination, inaction, and bottlenecks. Of course, high-quality work is important and always the goal; but if you wait to do things until conditions are perfect, you will produce less and miss important opportunities.

Bob fell into this time trap a lot. He procrastinated because he wanted to wait until he had enough time to focus on the problem or opportunity. Guess what? He never had enough time—and was never going to. He missed several opportunities because he was simply too picky and slow. Why was he like this? It was because he felt that if he were not perfect, his customers would not value him. Though his internal and external customers wanted high-quality work, what they missed most from Bob and his team was action and results.

Lonny knew that several members of his team were not performing adequately. But each time his manager talked with him about this, he had another reason why the time was not right to make the necessary changes. The busy season was coming up, and he didn't have time to train new employees. His team had recently lost a member, so he couldn't afford to make any changes in personnel. There was a new supervisor on the team, and Lonny wanted to see if his employees might respond to this new person more favorably—and on and on. Each excuse may have been valid, but together they formed a pattern of inaction and demonstrated Lonny's hesitancy to take care of the problem. The conditions were never going to be perfect for him to take control of the situation and make the necessary changes. Eventually, he was fired and replaced by a manager who was willing to be more proactive.

If you're one of those middle managers who has the tendency to wait too long to take action, a good mantra might be Shakespeare's famous line "He who hesitates is lost." Waiting until the timing is just right wastes time and slows down progress.

Fallacy 5: Slowing Down Decreases Output

In some cases, going slow is the best way to go faster. Ready, aim, fire. Slow, slow, fast. To achieve excellent results, it is best to complete a methodical, up-front analysis (slow), plan well (slow), and energetically implement (fast).

Middle managers who spend more time on up-front planning, building relationships, and ensuring that the work supports their goals will outpace and outperform those who rush things. In addition, pausing midstream to analyze how the work is going can create much-needed energy to move the work forward or facilitate a breakthrough.

At Black & Decker, one of the key factors that enabled the team to reduce the product development cycle for the DeWalt power tool line was investing more time up front. Black & Decker devoted more time to ensuring they knew the features and benefits each tool should have, and then to designing the tool for the highest quality and manufacturability. They also took time in the beginning to do some team training and role clarification, which improved productivity and communication during the project management phase. Because of the time allocated up front, they were able to shorten the product development cycle by months.

Be aware, however, that sometimes being slow is just taking too much time. The activities that take time up front but pay off in the end include good analysis, effective planning, clarifying expectations and roles, and relationship building. Middle managers who spend more time doing these things will find that their throughput improves.

Letting Go of the Victim Mentality

The five fallacies about time prevent middle managers from making the most of their day. Another significant barrier that reduces your effectiveness is "victim conversations" about time. A victim conversation is something you say or think that has a "woe is me" quality to it. When it comes to time, a victim conversation might sound like this:

I am so busy, I can't think straight.
I don't have time for this.
Another day is gone and I didn't put a dent into my to-do list.

Debbie was a big whiner when it came to time. Although she had a huge job and many time-related challenges, her victim conversations got in her way more than all her other challenges put together. Her victim conversations kept her from taking action and stopped her from thinking creatively. When she thought or spoke about her frustrations about time, in that moment, she made it impossible to progress. Think about how ridiculous these complaints sound:

> I can't believe the day is already half over. I have not spent five minutes at my desk all day. I do not know when I am going to be able to get this done. I would not wish this job on my enemy.

How can anything productive follow statements like these? When people like Debbie habitually gripe about not having enough time, they are sealing their fate and making their problem worse. Venting frustrations now and then is natural, but when it is a common response, the victim conversation becomes a major barrier to success.

High-Impact Middle Management Techniques for Mastering Time

High-impact middle managers have beaten the time demons and learned to make wise choices about how to spend their day. They know that managing time well will enable them to work more on meaningful projects and establish the better work/life balance needed for them to stay sane and happy. The high-impact middle management techniques for mastering time include

- Perform periodic time audits.
- Set the pace.
- Apply the 80/20 rule to choices about time.
- Use tiny pockets of time to get big results.
- Plan, plan, plan.

In addition, these managers have come to know that their good time management habits have rubbed off on their team members. High-impact middle managers lead by example. Let's look at each of the five techniques listed just above.

Technique 1: Perform Periodic Time Audits

The best way for middle managers to determine how efficiently they use time is to complete a time audit. A time audit reveals the level of alignment that exists between the middle manager's goals and how he or she spends time. Unlike other time inventories, the time audit does not seek to detail how a manager spends each minute. The time audit focuses on the type of activity, not each specific action. Not only would it take too much time to complete a detailed inventory, it is also unnecessary. To perform a time audit, complete exercise 9-1.

The time audit emphasizes the things that are most important for a middle manager to devote his or her time to. Here are a few suggestions for each part of the time audit given in exercise 9-1.

Time Audit: Part 1

Part 1 is a place to establish what the priorities should be. It is important to take the time to fill out this part so the answers can be referred to during the other parts of the audit. In addition, the act of summarizing the priorities will help middle managers focus on them.

Time Audit: Part 2

Middle managers should spend at least 75 percent of their time, or six hours a day, on the work described in part 1. It is important to make sure the actions are not only aligned to goals, but that they are also the best choices from many possible actions. For example, asking a peer about a concern may support resolving the concern, but is this action going to make a difference? Would calling a meeting and brainstorming potential solutions be a better use of the same time?

Middle managers tend to spend too much time in meetings. It is valuable to question the meetings attended and their effectiveness. If a meeting is not effective, ask the meeting leader to make positive changes; or stop attending, if possible.

Middle managers need to focus on enabling their employees to perform their best. Many busy middle managers allow their attention to get diverted by the needs of the day and may go months without thinking about how to coach and facilitate performance. Ideally, optimizing individual and team performance, as identified in part 1, is a top priority. If not, it should be added to the list.

It is also important for you to feel comfortable that your management peers and employees would agree that you are spending time in

Exercise 9-1. Perform a Time Audit

Part 1	Response
My broad goals, based on my manager's expectations, are . . .	
My most important priorities are . . .	
I am most concerned about . . .	
The barriers getting in the way of my team's productivity are . . .	
Planning and analysis that I need to complete in the next month . . .	

Part 2	Response
The approximate percentage of my time spent on items described in part 1 is . . .	
Are the actions I am taking adding value?	
The average number of hours a week I have spent in meetings is . . .	
Are these meetings a good use of my time? Why? / Why not?	
Which meetings should I keep and which should I no longer go to?	
Are the meetings well run and effective?	
How successful are my employees? What have I done to optimize their performance?	
How clear is my team about which tasks are of highest priority?	
If I shared how I spend my time with my manager, peers, and employees, what would they likely say?	
How much time over the last week did I spend doing versus managing?	
How many hours do I work on average?	

Part 3	Response
Based on this audit, what goals should I set to improve how I spend time?	
What beliefs should I take on to help support these goals?	
What immediate actions can I take to begin using my time more wisely?	

Note: A full-size version is available for download at www.lisahaneberg.com.

the ways that matter most. If you don't think they would agree with your choices, then expectations and priorities might need to be realigned and you might need to say "no" more often. Overall, middle managers should be able to gain support and agreement that they are working on the tasks that are most important and beneficial.

It is important to notice if doing gets more attention than managing, and why. If so, is it because doing is more comfortable and satisfying?

Middle managers who work more than 40 hours a week, on average, should look at how they spend their time and ensure that they get the most value out of each hour worked. Managers who work more than 60 hours a week are not managing their time well and should seek to reduce the number of hours worked while improving productivity.

Time Audit: Part 3

Beliefs that could help you manage your time might include statements like "As a middle manager, I am expected to optimize individual and team performance and I need to be spending more time focusing on this to meet this expectation and responsibility"; or "Right now the top priority is planning for the coming busy season. Time spent working on this now will benefit my team and me later. I need to make sure that nothing gets in the way of this important planning."

Be bold and assertive when making your list of immediate actions to take to improve time management, because doing so will be more energizing and empowering. "I don't know" is not an acceptable answer to this question. The list should contain at least 10 possible actions.

The time audit is useful for determining the alignment that exists between how a middle manager spends his or her time and the most important results. If you find you are spending too much time on tasks not listed in part 1 of the time audit, try to resist the urge to rationalize or make excuses. Though it is true that most middle managers face dozens of requests a day for their time, it is your responsibility to determine the best method to get the work completed. Middle managers need to be able to decline requests that get in the way of work that should be their top priority.

Technique 2: Set the Pace

Middle managers determine the pace of the organization. "Pace" is the rate at which work proceeds, but it is also the rate at which a person walks. For middle managers, both definitions are important. To establish and maintain an electric, exciting, and productive pace within which it feels good to work, the pace of the work and the people needs to be brisk. In a work environment like this, workers feel like making things happen and they accomplish more. Intel and Amazon.com are examples of companies with a brisk pace; there is nothing lethargic about their work environments! People walk down the hallways with determination and speed. They are clearly thinking about something. Within earshot are two people engaged in a lively discussion about how to solve a problem. In a meeting room, a manager is drawing a diagram on the white board, arrows going everywhere, heads nodding.

Although both Intel and Amazon.com are high-technology companies and might be expected to have a fast-paced environment, that is not why their work pace is fast. It is brisk because their middle managers make it so. Any workplace, even a 125-year-old paper mill, can have an exciting pace if the middle managers create that type of environment. Here's how to create pace:

- *Manage by walking around.* It does not do any good if you only leave your desk once a day. Managers who circulate and talk to their people, as well as those in other departments and their managers, are informed, perceived as accessible, and create a positive energy in the office.
- *Initiate action every day.* Get moving on projects or ideas that are on the to-do list. Do not allow procrastination to get in the way of action.
- *Facilitate meetings and ask people to participate* (as opposed to meetings where the leader speaks and everyone else just sits there). Facilitate brainstorming or problem-solving sessions on a regular basis.
- *Ask people for their ideas every day.*
- *Express a sense of urgency that comes from being excited about the work.*

- *Celebrate successes and create anticipation for future successes.*
- *Have fun at work.* Smile and laugh. Take the work seriously, but enjoy it, too.
- *Make the removal of barriers and mucky-muck a top priority.* Don't let anything get in the way of your team's progress.

Tim, a middle manager at a software company, was always on the move. Striding down the hallway, he looked like a man with a mission. But anyone could still stop him and strike up a conversation. He would jump into the conversation with fervor and interest. He always worked at a brisk pace and emitted a focused energy that was contagious to others in his area. He would share at least one new idea daily. To his boss, Tim was a bit of a nuisance, but in a good way. His employees began thinking more quickly, too. Within three months, he had improved the pace of his new department by being an outstanding role model and encouraging a fun and lively work environment.

Technique 3: Apply the 80/20 Rule to Choices about Time

The time audit reveals whether or not you are spending your time on work that matters. As a middle manager, you can use the 80/20 rule to help make wise choices about how you use your time. Of all the items on an average daily to-do list, 20 percent are critical. This 20 percent produces 80 percent of the results. A high-impact middle manager identifies and focuses on this 20 percent. When the fire drills of the day begin to usurp time, high-impact middle managers prioritize the 20 percent of the work that needs to remain the focus. If something in the schedule must be cut, high-impact middle managers make sure that it's not part of this 20 percent.

Case Study

Jim's responsibilities were undergoing a fundamental shift. Jim and his manager had agreed that Jim's top priority was to leverage signs of recovery in the market and focus on maximizing revenue for the company. Jim's job was to make sure that the company seized every available opportunity to increase revenues. Almost overnight, his focus changed. No longer would he spend time on any topic of discussion. He began entrusting his most competent managers with handling more issues and decisions without him. He let his staff know that he was going to back out of selected meetings and spend more time focusing on tasks that were aligned with his new mandate. His direct and forthcoming approach worked. His managers quickly adjusted to the level and type of involvement that were being asked of them. He learned that the best way to improve how he spent his time was to first make different and better choices, then clearly and openly communicate these changes to team members and peers. To keep himself on track, he would ask himself if the task he was working on was going to have an impact on revenue. If not, he would delegate the task to focus his time on his most critical objective: generating revenue.

Sometimes, middle managers think that if they work harder, they will be able to accomplish their goals. Often, however, the most important choice they make is about what they will do, not how hard they will work. This point is illustrated in a short parable offered by Ralph Stayer:

> I'm sitting in a quiet room at the Millcroft Inn, a peaceful little place hidden back among the pine trees about an hour out of Toronto. It's just past noon, late July, and I'm listening to the desperate sounds of a life or death struggle going on a few feet away.
>
> There's a small fly burning out the last of its short life's energies in a futile attempt to fly through the glass of the windowpane. The whining wings tell the poignant story of the fly's strategy—try harder.
>
> But it's not working.
>
> The frenzied effort offers no hope for survival. Ironically, the struggle is part of the trap. It is impossible for the fly to try hard enough to succeed at breaking through the glass. Nevertheless, this little insect has staked its life on reaching its goal through raw effort and determination.
>
> The fly is doomed. It will die there on the windowsill.
>
> Across the room, 10 steps away, the door is open. Ten seconds of flying time and this small creature could reach the outside world it seeks. With only a fraction of the effort now being wasted, it

could be free of this self-imposed trap. The breakthrough possibility is there. It would be so easy.

Why doesn't the fly try another approach, something dramatically different? How did it get so locked in on the idea that this particular route and determined effort offer the most promise for success? What logic is there in continuing until death, to seek a breakthrough with "more of the same"? No doubt, this approach makes sense to the fly. Regrettably, it's an idea that will kill.

Trying harder and harder is an approach that makes sense to many middle managers. Unfortunately, it often leads to burnout rather than success. Trying harder isn't necessarily the way to achieve more. It may not offer any real promise for getting what you want out of life. Sometimes, in fact, it's a big part of the problem. If you stake your hopes for a breakthrough on trying harder than ever, you may kill your chances for success.

Creating Work/Life Balance

In his best-selling book *Maverick: The Success Story Behind the World's Most Unusual Workplace*, Ricardo Semler, the well-known and highly regarded CEO of Semco in Brazil, had this to say about the importance of handling time: "I took sixteen aspirins in just one day. Before I could reorganize Semco, I had to reorganize myself. Long hours were the first issue I tackled. They were one of the biggest symptoms of time sickness, a disease that afflicts far too many executives. So I set 7 p.m. as the time I would leave the office, no matter what. After that, I would go to the movies, read books (but not business books)—anything but work. I wouldn't do any work on the weekends, either.... Yes, I would attack my problem directly, and that problem was not simply the management of a business but something even more fundamental: the management of time."

Many managers suffer from what Semler calls time sickness. They equate quality with quantity and attack work backlogs with a try-harder mentality. This approach is a recipe for burnout and failure. High-impact middle managers have learned that managing time enables many other successes to occur.

Technique 4: Use Tiny Pockets of Time to Get Big Results

It is 8:53 a.m. and there is a meeting scheduled to begin at 9:00. Brett has prepared for the meeting, and the needed materials have been copied and organized and ready to distribute. What should he do now? There isn't enough time to start anything new—or is there? Glancing quickly at his to-do list, he gets up and seeks out one of his employees. He asks a few questions, clarifies what needs to occur, and asks the employee to follow up with peers in another department. Returning to his desk, he grabs his materials and several other items to drop off in the mailroom on the way to the meeting. In the hall outside the meeting, he chats with a peer and resolves an open issue on his to-do list. He quickly lets his employees know that they can immediately act on the information instead of waiting until the meeting is over. He is still among the first to arrive at the meeting, and in seven minutes, has accomplished three tasks that will help his team members work more effectively.

High-impact middle managers routinely use tiny pockets of time to accomplish tasks on their to-do lists. It's all too easy to waste the few minutes before meetings or appointments. Most people figure there is not enough time to start anything big, so why bother? There are two reasons that using these small amounts of time wisely will pay off. First, and most obviously, middle managers who use this time wisely will get more work done. If the average middle manager has five segments in their day, and the manager completes a couple of tasks before each segment begins, that's 10 additional tasks completed each day! Second, and just as important, doing things in these small bits of time energizes you and keeps you on pace. Conversely, wasting time scatters motivation and energy. Tasks that lend themselves to this practice include

- checking in with an employee
- asking a peer for clarification
- reading a quick article or memo
- sharing information
- requesting a report or information for analysis to be done later
- returning a phone call
- filling out paperwork that has been sitting in your inbox too long

- sending out a meeting appointment and creating the agenda
- managing by walking around.

Middle managers can use tiny pockets of time to facilitate a breakthrough. Taking 10 minutes to ask new, open-ended questions can spur fresh thinking about how to solve an old problem. It takes just a few moments to create and deliver several new questions verbally or by email. If the questions help move the problem or project forward, these 10 minutes may prove to be the most valuable time you spend all day.

Technique 5: Plan, Plan, Plan

Most middle managers do not spend enough time planning. Often, they opt to deal with the tyranny of the urgent and let planning slide. This strategy is rarely effective, because it begins a vicious cycle of not spending time on the right tasks, because there is no good work plan, because there is no time to plan, and so on. Each day, middle managers should take a few minutes to plan their day. Weekly and monthly planning is equally as important. (Techniques for creating excellent work plans can be found in chapter 7.)

Planning can be a therapeutic practice for middle managers who worry that there is too much to do. Concerns about remembering what is most important and what might happen if something falls through the cracks are allayed when a good plan is in place. With a good work plan, you can breathe easier, because the most important work will be at the top of the list. Even though a work plan may be daunting and contain a long list of tasks, having a plan is always more comforting than worrying about "what-if" scenarios.

Middle managers who do not make good choices about how to spend their time will likely suffer from career setbacks, a poor work/life balance, and suboptimal results. To the casual observer, they may appear scattered and overwhelmed. Conversely, those who ensure their time is focused on doing the right things in an efficient manner will experience more success and satisfaction. They will appear to be on top of things and confident. High-impact middle managers have time to get their jobs done and be accessible and responsive to team members and peers. These effective managers periodically review how they are spending their time and ensure that they have their priorities straight. For the busy middle manager, time is a precious commodity that needs to be proactively and effectively utilized.

Case Study

Todd was an excellent planner. Fortunately, this skill rubbed off on his peers. In work sessions or meetings, he would frequently ask "What's the plan?" or "Do we have a plan for how we are going to accomplish this?" He would ask questions that slowed the group down and made them focus on the tasks involved, each person's role in the project, and due dates. This process prevented Todd and his team from overcommitting. He knew that taking the time to talk through the planning for each major project would serve him and his colleagues well in the end. His excellent planning helped them execute tasks more effectively. His work was never late. He managed his day to ensure that he completed the most important work first. When he committed to do something, people knew they could count on him to deliver.

Part IV

Performance Leadership: Ensuring That Team Members Excel in Execution

Chapter 10

Performance Management Myths: What Not to Do

M ike complained that he wasn't able to spend much time managing his people because he had too many other important tasks to do. He did not enjoy having performance conversations or team meetings and generally tried to avoid them. Meanwhile, his two teams were struggling with different performance challenges. One team employed many smart and hardworking people who were overwhelmed by ambiguous roles and turnover within the department. The other team lacked focus and had several people who were not a good fit for their respective positions. Both teams lacked effective and proactive management. Compounding the problem was the fact that many members of Mike's staff had become helpless while working for three ineffective managers over the last five years.

Mike found his team's performance unsatisfactory, but his assumptions about management were getting in the way of his correcting the problem. First, optimizing individual performance does not take much time. Mike spent more time than he would have spent optimizing his team members' performance reacting to problems that wouldn't have occurred if he had spent more time managing well from the beginning. Second, his belief that managing performance was secondary to his other work handicapped his effectiveness. One of the most important contributions a middle manager can make is to ensure that his or her teams are performing well and getting results. Mike thought that if he ignored the problem long enough, it would fix itself, go away, or become someone else's problem. Those beliefs were not helping him solve the performance problems within his teams. He needed to replace those management assumptions with more helpful ones.

The High-Impact Middle Management System helps middle managers optimize performance by clarifying which actions improve performance and which do not. The system then focuses on developing the skills needed to carry out the most worthwhile practices. As with many areas of management, the 80/20 rule applies. There are a few managerial habits (the 20 percent) that will make the greatest impact (the 80 percent) on individual performance. To get to the 20 percent, it is first important to understand the management assumptions that are not helpful and the actions that either work poorly or do not work at all (the 80 percent of actions that yield only 20 percent of results).

Five Myths about Managing People

At one time, many scientists thought the world was flat. Ten years ago, most people could not have conceived of using cellphones to take pictures and play games. The medical community is continually revising its list of foods that are healthy and those that are not. Each year, science and industry learn new and better ways to solve problems and get things done. During the last 50 years, what is known and believed about management has been changing as well. These five myths about managing people are examples of where research and experience indicate a change in perspectives and practices is warranted:

- Employees do not want management.
- Performance evaluation systems improve performance.
- Employees prefer a sugarcoated counseling session to a candid one.

- Positive reinforcement is a great tool for improving performance.
- Salary increases improve employee motivation and productivity.

Let's look at each myth.

Myth 1: Employees Do Not Want Management

It might be true that employees dislike micromanagement, but it is not correct to assume that employees do not want to work in a well-managed department. Employees who work for poor managers often feel frustrated, lost, unfocused, and unsuccessful. They may even feel abandoned. Employees expect and hope that their manager will show leadership, plan the work, and make sure that everyone is doing his or her job. They want their manager to ensure that the team is working on the right tasks and is aware of changes that are happening within the department and the organization. Employees want to know whether their work is satisfactory and whether there are performance concerns, and, if so, to be told about them honestly and in a timely fashion. If something is wrong, employees want their managers to have the courage and conviction to deal with it quickly. This includes dealing with nonperformers who are not pulling their weight. Employees do not respect managers who don't or won't manage.

Case Study

Jim terminated Jane because she did not manage well. Senior managers worried her employees would be angry and upset when they learned of the news. Jane was fun, friendly, and well liked. Much to the senior manager's surprise, Jane's employees were not angry. Though they felt sad for Jane, they knew from firsthand experience that she was not a good functional manager and saw her departure as an opportunity to bolster the team's success. Her replacement experienced little resistance, and many employees asked why it took senior management so long to make the change.

Employees recognize that it is their manager's responsibility to be proactive and a leader in ensuring that all team members are performing.

Employees do not want to feel as though they are being managed in a controlling or dogmatic way, but an effective, functional management style is both desired and expected.

Myth 2: Performance Evaluation Systems Improve Performance

In his classic book *Out of the Crisis*, the quality expert W. Edwards Deming called performance evaluation systems one of the deadly diseases of Western management. Alfie Kohn, a university professor and expert on human behavior, said in his book *Punished by Rewards*, "Even if performance appraisals were adequate to gauge how well people are doing, their effects are usually so destructive that they shouldn't be used anyway." Management and quality consultant Peter Scholtes had this to say in his article "Performance without Appraisal":

> For most people, either giving or receiving a performance appraisal is like a visit to the dentist: it is not fun, but it is good for you. Here is some news for you: performance appraisal is not good for you. Performance appraisal, when looked at more deeply, not only does no good, it does harm. Performance appraisal, in fact, is a flat-out disaster, a virus that is going to damage our organizations and our people.... Performance appraisal is an example of the old philosophy. It is a remnant of obsolescence which clings like a parasite, draining energy from our organizations.

The management consultant and writer Peter Block shares Scholtes's sentiment about performance appraisal: "Sold as a developmental experience, I think the real function of performance appraisal and its derivatives is more about maintaining control. It is a time, once a year, when we are reminded by our boss and the institution that they own us."

Performance evaluations do not improve performance. This may seem like a bizarre statement in light of the fact that most every company uses an appraisal system to manage performance. Could all these organizations be wrong? In their book *Abolishing Performance Appraisals*, Tom Coens and Mary Jenkins point out that the research shows that performance evaluations do not work:

Our harsh censure of appraisal rests on a solid foundation. Academia, industry, and professional associations have intensely scrutinized appraisal for more than 50 years now, producing hundreds of studies, surveys, and articles. Despite a strong bias by many researchers who favor appraisal or imply that appraisal is indispensable, these studies and surveys offer scant evidence of appraisal's success.

Many companies, middle managers, and indeed managers at all levels want to believe that their evaluation systems are worth the time and effort. Although it may make intuitive sense to review performance once or twice a year, the evidence that performance evaluations are not effective is clear. Why? It is clear for the simple reason that in most companies, managers dread doing performance evaluations and employees dislike receiving them.

Moreover, many evaluations are not accurate. Few employees receive a truthful review, because their managers would rather deliver a positive evaluation. One reason for this is that managers do not want employees to think their performance is negative or lacking. This makes for an awkward and uncomfortable conversation that many managers would prefer to avoid. And managers may grade an employee's performance as higher than it actually is for a second reason: because they do not want to hurt their employee's chances of getting a raise or promotion.

Although there are significant differences in how performance evaluation systems work, the results of studies are similar. Even companies that use detailed and structured evaluation systems have been largely unable to show a link between the evaluation process and performance improvement. Those who favor evaluation systems often cite these reasons:

- The evaluation system documents performance and provides a paper trail in case of legal issues in the future (like a wrongful termination suit).
- The evaluation system identifies high and low performers. The evaluation process weeds out poor performers. Top performers get the recognition they deserve when they receive an outstanding evaluation.

- The evaluation process ensures that managers have formal performance conversations with their employees.
- The evaluation system promotes discussions that clarify the expectations managers have of their employees.

These beliefs may be true but, interestingly enough, they do not directly foster improved performance—except in the case of the last point. Though it is important for employees to be clear about expectations, relying on a performance evaluation session to accomplish this is not wise. Because both the manager and the employee want to get the evaluation conversation over with as soon possible, it is unlikely that any high-quality discussion is going to occur. Even top performers usually prefer to skip the formal evaluation discussion.

Why use unpopular, ill-designed, and fruitless performance evaluation systems? Along with being ineffective, evaluation systems also take up substantial time and resources. Middle managers should not rely on a performance evaluation process to help improve individual or team performance. Techniques for improving performance are the focus of chapter 11.

Myth 3: Employees Prefer a Sugarcoated Counseling Session to a Candid One

Middle managers who fail to get to the point and do not have the courage to speak plainly and candidly put their employees through an experience that they should not have to endure. Employees know when their manager is dancing around a subject or putting a positive spin on an otherwise negative message. It is more effective (and humane) to communicate the concern in specifics and without any sugarcoating.

Case Study

Everyone agreed that Mindy was a great person and hard worker, but not a good manager of people. When Jim went to Mindy to discuss his concern that she was not ensuring that her managers were working on the right tasks, Jim danced around the topic. He recognized that Mindy was busy, and he said he knew she meant well and tried hard and that her situation was unenviable. He expressed the concerns he had about her managers' productivity and why he felt this way. However, he did not clearly communicate the concerns that he had about her performance. He should have told her that her performance was not satisfactory, that she had not been managing her managers attentively, and that he expected her to fix the problem. When he left her office, she felt stressed, frustrated, and unsure of what he expected her to do. Throughout the conversation, she could tell that he was dancing around the topic and wished he would get to the point and not make it drag on any longer.

Many good managers falter when it comes to counseling their employees effectively. Managers will often sandwich criticism between positive statements so the employee will not feel badly or react poorly. The sandwich technique doesn't work, however, because employees see right through the effort and don't focus on the important points conveyed. If a middle manager needs to counsel an employee, he or she should do so in a manner that is direct, clear, and candid.

Myth 4: Positive Reinforcement Is a Great Tool for Improving Performance

Suzy had just received another "atta girl" from her manager for perfect attendance. Yesterday it was for getting the project done on time. Her manager was always praising her for one thing or another. All this positive reinforcement should have made her feel great, but it didn't.

Many positive reinforcement practices backfire because they manage behavior, not optimize performance. Behavior modification, popularized by the psychologist B. F. Skinner in the 1930s and 1940s, is a practice that works to shape and mold behavior. The basic idea is that when employees receive positive reinforcement, they are more likely to repeat the behaviors that elicited the praise. Conversely, negative reinforcement will cause an employee to engage in a particular behavior less often. Management training programs that teach this technique often recommend delivering positive reinforcement fives times more frequently than negative reinforcement. Some even ask managers to keep tick sheets to record the positive reinforcement they dole out.

Here's the problem: When positive reinforcement is part of a deliberate practice, it feels fake and manipulative. Employees can see through these techniques and end up feeling insulted rather than motivated. Managing by positive reinforcement is a practice that affects an employee's extrinsic motivation but rarely improves his or her intrinsic motivation. In fact, employees who work in an environment heavily laden with positive reinforcement will likely find work less intrinsically motivating. Tapping into an employee's intrinsic motivation is a better way to improve performance. (Strategies for improving intrinsic motivation appear later in this chapter.)

For example, coming to work on time because you know that if you don't you will be reprimanded is an example of being extrinsically motivated. You are motivated to do something because of what you will receive (positive or negative) as a result. Intrinsic motivation is a drive that comes from within and is based on a personally held value, belief, or goal. Extrinsic motivation is compliance based; intrinsic motivation is interest based. Positive reinforcement systems improve extrinsic motivation but not intrinsic motivation. Managers who want to maximize performance will be more successful if they create an environment where intrinsic motivation is improved, because this is where employee passion, drive, creativity, and energy come from.

It is important to distinguish positive reinforcement from appreciation. Employees do want to feel appreciated and that they make a difference. They want their managers to value and listen to them. Practicing positive reinforcement does not accomplish this.

Myth 5: Salary Increases Improve Employee Motivation and Productivity

At one company, salary increases occurred at the same time of the year for everyone. If salary increases improve employee motivation, one would have expected to see productivity go up after the raises took effect. Of course, this did not happen. In fact, there was no observable difference in performance or the employees' dispositions. The industrial psychologist Frederick Hertzberg studied the factors that bring about job satisfaction and dissatisfaction. He identified two groups of factors that affect employee satisfaction: hygiene factors and motivators. Hygiene factors include work conditions, pay, status, and security. When hygiene factors are poor, work is dissatisfying. When hygiene factors are acceptable, work is not dissatisfying. Adding more hygiene factors beyond what is satisfactory does not increase employee motivation.

Hertzberg's motivators influence employee satisfaction based on the fulfillment of intrinsic, or higher-level, needs. These needs include achievement, recognition, the quality of the work itself, and an opportunity for growth. Motivators improved worker satisfaction much more than hygiene factors alone ever could.

Case Study

Harry's team was in danger of losing several key members. Harry felt that to keep these talented managers, he would need to give them salary adjustments. However, what concerned the managers most was Harry's inconsistent and poor leadership. They wanted him to represent their needs to senior managers and thought he did not manage the department well. These managers were due for a raise and deserved one, but that was not the primary reason several were thinking of leaving the company. These managers were experiencing a great deal of daily hassles, which were sapping them of much of their intrinsic motivation.

Hertzberg's theory explained something that managers have seen in practice. Pay and other extrinsic rewards do not improve performance, nor do they increase an employee's overall motivation. When lacking, or at an unsatisfactory level, these extrinsic factors can get in the way of employee motivation; but once they are at a satisfactory level, they have little impact on motivation or achievement.

The performance management practices described in the context of the five myths outlined above damage individual and team performance. They stem from a command-and-control mindset about how to manage people. High-impact middle managers know that tapping into their employee's hearts and minds is significantly more productive and fun. They know that employees want them to be great managers and to communicate with them in a manner that is straightforward and authentic. Employees want to be appreciated and included in meaningful brainstorming and problem-solving discussions. High-impact middle managers know that these things matter much more than gold stars, performance ratings, and other extrinsic rewards. The five myths about managing people illustrate what not to do to improve performance. Techniques for maximizing performance and satisfaction are offered in chapter 11.

Chapter 11

Using High-Impact Middle Management Principles to Optimize Individual Performance

The five myths about managing people presented in chapter 10 described managerial practices that do not work. In addition to not being effective, these common practices are very labor and time intensive. There is a better way for middle managers to optimize individual performance! To encourage and facilitate great team member performance, middle managers need to understand and employ techniques based on beliefs about what it takes to encourage peak performance in others. High-impact middle managers spend their management time in productive ways that yield better results. They focus on the few performance-optimizing practices that offer the greatest benefits. And although middle managers are managers, the best do not manage people in the common sense of the word "management." They manage work flow, processes, systems, and communication. They enable their employees but do not manage them. To optimize performance, your goals should be to

1. Make sure that the work gets done well and on time.
2. Ensure that the right people are in the right jobs.
3. Facilitate an environment where improvement and creativity are encouraged.

Middle managers who select the right people, support them, and clearly communicate expectations will find that their employees, by and large, will manage themselves on a day-to-day basis. What employees need most is for their managers to clear the way so they can do their best work. To accomplish these objectives, middle managers should focus on these five high-impact middle management principles for optimizing individual performance:

1. Ensure that everyone knows what he or she is expected to achieve.
2. Have regular conversations about how each employee is meeting expectations in clear and simple terms.
3. Follow principles 1 and 2 in ways that maximize intrinsic motivation.
4. Take decisive and proactive action to deal with poor performers.
5. Be selective when hiring. Do not settle for someone who is not the right fit for the position or team.

Let's look at each of these principles.

Performance Principle 1: Ensure That Everyone Knows What He or She Is Expected to Achieve

As a middle manager, you can immediately improve the focus and productivity of your team members by ensuring that they know what is expected of them. When high-impact middle managers talk with their employees, they go beyond discussing obvious expectations. They ensure that each person has a good understanding of how he or she can best contribute to the company. Notice the significant difference between the list of expectations discussed by most managers and that discussed by high-impact middle managers.

The usual expectations conversation includes

- required tasks
- project work
- the types of tasks that this person should own
- the expectation that the employee will bring questions and problems to the manager.

The high-impact middle management expectations conversation also includes expectations about

- how this person should contribute to identifying and solving problems
- how this person will represent his or her function and the company
- generating new ideas and improving results
- how this employee should analyze and manage organizational resources (for example, staff, finances, and equipment)
- how this person will manage employees
- the business relationships this person should maintain and develop
- deadlines, execution, and results
- judgment and decisions
- meeting preparedness and participation
- planning and communicating work
- how this person needs to improve his or her performance— for example, "Over the next year, I would like to see you more closely manage productivity in the A/P area and improve the speed and accuracy of the employees of that area. This is an area where you have not been as attentive or effective."

The second list of expectations conversation topics may seem long, but it is necessary to ensure that each person fully understands what he or she is expected to accomplish. Middle managers who use this method of setting expectations will notice an immediate and welcome difference in their employees' focus, because this approach fully communicates the breadth and importance of each person's role. Some employees may initially find this daunting or overwhelming; however, the ones who truly want to excel and do high-quality work will find this clarification of expectations motivating.

Do not get too prescriptive when discussing expectations. For example, it can be helpful to let the employee know how often he or she should provide progress updates. It is not helpful to define what the planning report should look like, how to disseminate work assignments, or the list of tasks to be included in the first report. That is micromanagement.

Expectations conversations establish the measuring stick for performance, not the blueprint for how the employee is to conduct his or her work. If the employee could use a few tips on how to accomplish a task or project, schedule a separate coaching discussion to address this need.

A successful discussion will set up a powerful foundation for optimal performance and productivity. Clearly communicating expectations accomplishes more than any other performance management activity and is at the top of the 80/20 list of great and right work to do.

Before the discussion:

- Think about and write down expectations. Type them up and make a copy to share with the employee.
- Talk with peers and other managers to ensure that assumptions about improvement areas are correct.
- Schedule the meeting at a time that is conducive to a relaxed and thorough discussion (not 30 minutes before a big meeting, or at 4:30 p.m. on a Friday).
- Let the employee know that this discussion will focus on ensuring that he or she is clear about what is expected and how he or she can make a significant contribution to the company. Explain that clarifying expectations helps managers stay focused and successful, and that other staff members will be scheduled for similar conversations.

During the discussion:

- This is no time to be wimpy or general—share expectations in clear, specific, and resolute terms. Cover all the areas, and more, on the high-impact middle management list that are applicable to this person's job.
- Express expectations in a "matter-of-fact" manner. This is important to reduce the emotional content of the discussion. An expectations conversation should not become a sermon, plea, or sales pitch.
- Focus on the essential outcome—but allow some latitude on how to get there.
- Never assume that expectations are clear. Cover all expectations.

- Answer requests for clarification, but do not allow the meeting to creep into other topics. The desired outcome of this discussion is that expectations are clear and understood.

After the discussion:

- Once the initial discussion has taken place, expectations can be reinforced in a variety of day-to-day settings. Doing so will also help others in the organization understand each person's role and responsibilities.
- Be sure to follow up on expectations that are not being met. Do not wait to address concerns or issues, because doing so implies that it was not really an expectation.

Many employees do not fully understand what is expected of them, which is a shame, because it impairs satisfaction, productivity, and results. By using these suggestions for clarifying expectations, you can ensure that your employees are focused on the right objectives and set up for success.

Performance Principle 2: Have Regular Conversations about How the Employee Is or Is Not Meeting Expectations

Many middle managers are uncomfortable with and fear providing performance feedback. This discomfort becomes greater when they need to address inadequate performance. Managing performance is a fundamental responsibility for all middle managers and yet is the most dreaded and most often ignored. Talking with people about their performance can be awkward and scary, but there are rewards for getting past the discomfort. Productivity, efficiency, teamwork, employee satisfaction, and retention improve with effective performance management.

One of the primary reasons that performance discussions are awkward is that they can be emotional. Don't try to make the message more palatable by stretching out the discussion or trying to be the employee's friend. Neither should you go to the other end of the toughness spectrum and come across as cold, hard-hitting, and critical. Either approach will likely provoke an emotional response from the employee, who will hear the concerns as a personal assault and become defensive, angry, guilty, sad, or anxious.

Another reason managers hesitate to provide performance feedback is that they may feel uncomfortable being the leader. Talking with employees about what they are not doing well can make you feel like their parent or superior, which can be undesirable and unpleasant.

The recommended process for discussing poor performance focuses on the exchange of simple, clear, and direct information that, it is hoped, leads to a mutual understanding of the situation and what is needed in the future. This process limits emotional content and stresses improvement and success. This process minimizes the controlling, or boss-like, attributes of most feedback and emphasizes collaboration. It is easier for the middle manager who must deliver the message and more favorable to the employee who must receive it.

High-impact middle managers know how to discuss performance concerns in a matter-of-fact way that is quick, to the point, and clear. They talk with their employees about what is working and what isn't. Though some performance concerns will warrant a dedicated meeting, daily discussions usually suffice for dealing with most concerns. The less it looks or feels like an event or scolding, the more effective the discussion will be. The sidebar gives a few examples of what high-impact middle management performance conversations sound like.

Scenario #1: As Part of Normal Day-to-Day Conversation

MANAGER: Sue, let's chat about this morning's product review meeting. The meeting went on a bit too long and got off track in a few places; don't you agree?

SUE: Yeah, I was trying to control it, but you know how some of those folks are. . . .

MANAGER: Sure, there is always a good chance in a group that size that someone's going to get off topic. That's why I think it's important to have a detailed agenda, desired outcomes, and advance notice of how each member should contribute to the meeting. We've talked about your role in leading effective

SUE:

MANAGER:

SUE:

MANAGER:

meetings before, and I know you know what to do. You probably just ran out of time or forgot to do all the prep.

SUE: Yes, a lack of time is part of the reason; but I also thought the meeting was going to be more simple and straightforward than it was.

MANAGER: I can understand that, but meetings soak up a lot of time. Will you make sure that your preparation and management of next week's meeting are complete, so you can achieve the desired outcomes?

SUE: I will. I was planning on doing that for sure.

MANAGER: Terrific. Now do you have a few minutes to talk about Mexico? I'd like to get your ideas about how we might find a few new vendors. . . .

Scenario #2: A Scheduled Performance Conversation

MANAGER: Kay, I want to talk to you about the two-year vendor contracts. They were due two weeks ago, and I just learned that several are still outstanding. What is holding up the remaining contracts?

KAY: Well, as you know, I rely on the managers in each division to get their contracts in to me. I call them every few days, but some are just running behind.

MANAGER: We need vendor contracts for our budgeting process. I would have expected you to bring this delay to my attention before the deadline. You are responsible for delivering on this timeline, and you need to do whatever it takes to get as many of these contracts in as soon as possible. I would have liked to have helped you, but I didn't know there was a problem. Now that the deadline has passed, let's talk about what you can do to get the outstanding contracts in as soon as possible. Would you like my help now in brainstorming ideas, or would you prefer to think about it on your own and discuss it later this afternoon?

KAY: Let me think about it. I want to determine the issues affecting each contract first, because there might be different options for how to ensure their completion.

MANAGER: Great, my last meeting ends at 3:30; let's chat then. If you need someone to help you pull files, ask Denise. The project I have her working on is not as important as this. See you later.

Counseling conversations should not communicate to the employee that he or she is bad, lacking, or a disappointment. These are devastating remarks to hear from a manager and would make it difficult for any employee to focus on solving the problem. Discussing the reason an employee is not performing as expected can leave him or her feeling bad and may get in the way of conversations about how to fix the problem. The high-impact middle management method focuses on getting the employee into productive action and contains these elements:

1. a statement of the problem in factual terms ("Here's what happened and why it is of concern. . . . ")
2. the employee's acknowledgment of the problem
3. a reaffirmation of the performance expected and a request to solve the problem
4. a closing statement that shows there are no hard feelings, that this is not personal, and that support and help are available if needed.

Sue was a passionate and hardworking manager who got a bit emotional about her work. After the conversation with her manager in scenario 1 in the sidebar, it was clear that she needed to take a break before moving on to other topics of discussion. This was fine. She needed to think about the information and digest what she had heard. Middle managers need to be aware of what their employees need to be most productive. Different employees will have different needs. These techniques do not guarantee that the employee will not have an emotional reaction to the performance feedback, but they do lessen the possibility of this happening. In addition, employees will focus on fixing the problem and have a full understanding that it should not occur again.

The process for discussing outstanding performance also focuses on simple, clear, and direct information. When an employee has done a great job, it is important to convey genuine appreciation in a way that does not look or feel like the positive reinforcement discussed in chapter 10. In other words, express appreciation for work that makes a difference and is important. Here's how to express appreciation for a job well done:

- State specifically what the employee did well.
- Elaborate on the impact his or her work has had on the team and company.

- Highlight the skills or behaviors he or she used to do this work.
- Thank the person for making the team look good and for his or her hard work.
- Express personal gratitude.
- If possible or practical, ask him or her to share the achievement with others, either by presenting his or her work in a meeting or by leading a related project.
- Ask other managers (the next level of management or a peer middle manager whom this person's work affects) to express their gratitude as well.

Performance Principle 3: Follow Principles 1 and 2 in Ways That Maximize Intrinsic Motivation

To move from mediocre to outstanding performance, employees need to have their hearts and minds fully engaged in the work they are doing. Intrinsically motivated employees produce this kind of productivity. That being the case, it is important that middle managers lead in ways that do not unintentionally wreck their employees' intrinsic motivation. This happens most often with middle managers who micromanage or rule with an iron fist. These managers' employees feel manipulated and overmanaged, and this can kill any desire or passion they might have for the work.

Managers cannot control their employees, but they can establish a work environment that nurtures intrinsic motivation. There are two types of motivation: intrinsic and extrinsic. Intrinsic motivation comes from within the person and refers to motivation to engage in an activity for its own sake. Intrinsically motivated people work on tasks because they find them enjoyable, satisfying, or meaningful. Intrinsic motivation is the inclination to seek out and master challenges. Intrinsic motivation is what motivates employees to do something they are not required to do.

Extrinsic motivation is the drive to do a particular task as a means to an end. Extrinsically motivated employees put in effort to complete the work, because they believe that doing so will result in a bonus, raise in pay, or other desirable outcome. Extrinsic motivation can also be a result of a compliance-driven workplace. Controlling factors such as rule books, bureaucracy, and narrow job roles are extrinsically motivating. The problem with extrinsic motivation is that it produces the minimum performance required to get a reward or avoid a negative outcome such as a reprimand or job termination. Extrinsically motivated employees do not have their hearts and minds engaged in the work. It is common in business for managers to propose bonus structures and reward systems designed to improve performance, but this only works if performance is bad, and then it will only work to raise performance to a mediocre level.

High-impact middle managers develop a work environment that allows intrinsic motivation to flourish. The elements that promote intrinsic motivation include

1. work that is meaningful
2. a feeling of progress, of making a difference
3. having choices during and discretion over one's day
4. work that exercises and engages the mind
5. a feeling of ability and competence.

High-impact middle management techniques that stress these elements will naturally establish an intrinsically motivating workplace. To optimize your employees' intrinsic motivation, you can take these actions:

- Distribute the most interesting and challenging work among employees. Remember Jane? She kept the plum projects for herself and gave the average or boring assignments to her employees. This was a bad tactic, because it excluded her employees from taking part in the most interesting work and did not build her organization's capacity.
- Encourage idea generation and unique approaches to problem solving. Allowing employees to play an active role in improving the business provides a sense that their work makes a difference.
- Encourage peers to help one another and share best practices.
- As much as it is practical, allow employees to define how to do their work. Giving them the latitude to decide how they will complete tasks improves the perception that they have choices and can exercise discretion.

- Know what each employee's interests and passions are and offer him or her projects and tasks that tap into them.

- Ensure that all employees grow and stay engaged in their work. Learning new skills and using them can be intrinsically motivating.

- Communicate to employees the higher purpose and impact of the work they do.

- Allow employees to own whole tasks or projects instead of smaller parts.

- Empower employees to manage the piece of the business defined by their role. Resist the urge to step in and take over.

- Provide employees with the full information they need to be successful in their jobs. Communicate as much as is possible and appropriate.

- Celebrate achievements. Offer genuine acknowledgment to employees for outstanding work.

- Check out your own intrinsic motivation. Be an excellent role model and do whatever it takes to stay fully engaged in your work.

High-impact middle managers who check the pulse of their work environment regularly will ensure that it is enriching and stimulating. This makes a significant positive difference to the overall performance and morale of the team. Tapping into employees' intrinsic motivations is the only way to enjoy peak performance levels.

Performance Principle 4: Take Decisive and Proactive Action to Deal with Poor Performers

Jake was agonizing over what he had to do that morning. He was going to terminate one of his managers. Meg had worked for the company for three years. She was a hard worker but a poor manager and poor strategist. Her employees disliked working for her because she was abrasive and manipulative and she played favorites. Jake had talked with Meg many times about her management style and her lack of strategic vision. Each time, she would put a good effort in for a few days but then slip back into her old ways. Her termination was well overdue, but that didn't make it any easier for Jake. He preferred being the good guy, making people happy, and handing out opportunities—not taking them away.

After Meg left the building, it was as if a fog had lifted. Employees who were previously thinking about leaving the company felt a sense of hope. Not one person expressed regret that Meg had left the company. After seeing how the organization responded to Meg's departure, Jake kicked himself for waiting so long to take care of the problem.

Keeping a nonperformer on the team is one of the most damaging decisions a middle manager can choose. Not only are the tasks of that individual's position not being performed, but the productivity and morale of the entire organization are also affected. Although it may be difficult to let an employee go, it is more difficult to see the team and individual flounder.

As a high-impact middle manager, you should do everything you can to help each person succeed. However, when these efforts fail, and it is clear that the fit is not right, you must take quick and decisive action to get the person out of the organization. Work with the human resources department to make sure that the proper documentation and cause exist, and then terminate the person. The best thing for all concerned is to get the termination over with quickly, so everyone can move on.

Jim was in his office for a long time. He had begun the termination discussion with one of his employees over an hour ago, and there were no signs the conversation was ending. He was a deeply caring middle manager who did not know when to end a conversation. Many managers think it is humane to let the termination conversation drag on and get into a lot of detail, but that is usually a mistake. It is much more sensitive to keep the discussion short and focused. Effective termination discussions get to the point quickly and efficiently; here are several useful techniques:

- Let the person know that they are being terminated near the beginning of the conversation. Taking a lot of time to lead up to this point will only add to the stress, worry, and false hope of the employee. Letting the employee know he or she is terminated early in the conversation will speed up the time it is going to take the employee to process what is happening and be ready to discuss what is next.

- Speak in a tone that is matter-of-fact without being insensitive or uncaring. It is important to convey the decision without being emotional while communicating regret that the situation was not solvable.

- If the employee asks for another chance to improve his or her performance, hold firm by saying the decision is final and that it's in the best interests of all involved to part ways.

- Move the discussion as quickly as possible to a review of the termination terms, severance, and what is going to happen when the employee leaves this meeting. Offer choices for the employee to clear his or her belongings after hours to lessen the embarrassment and discomfort. Be as flexible with the terms and conditions as possible.

- Respect the person after he or she is gone by not bad-mouthing the person in front of others and by being respectful of what is said about his or her departure.

Most employees want to do a great job and can be significant team contributors. For the few employees who will not work out, speed of action and consummate professionalism will serve you and your department well in the long run.

Performance Principle 5: Be Selective When Hiring—Do Not Settle for Someone Who Is Not the Right Fit

One of the most effective ways to ensure that there will need to be few termination conversations is to hire the right people in the first place. Most terminations are the result of a poor fit with the position. The desire to fill the position may tempt busy middle managers to accept a marginal candidate, but this is never the best solution. Hiring decisions are extremely important, and high-impact middle managers keep their standards and expectations high. They know the best person is going to infuse the team with positive energy and valuable skills.

Peter Drucker, one of the world's most important management experts, said this about people decisions in his classic book *Management: Tasks, Responsibilities, Practices:*

The people decision signals to every manager of the organization what it is that management really wants, really values, really rewards. Placement and promotion are the most critical people decisions. They, above all, require careful thinking and clear policy and procedures, which live up to high standards of fairness and equity. They should never be made on the basis of opinions and on a man's "potential." They should always be based on the factual record of performance against explicit goals and objectives.

Drucker stressed what most middle managers have seen in the workplace: that people decisions matter and communicate to the rest of the organization what it is looking for from its employees.

Middle managers who have outstanding team members will have a different management experience than that of their peers who are not so lucky. Everything is easier, better, more fun, and more effective when dealing with high-performing individuals. The high-impact middle management techniques for hiring only the best include the following:

- Collaborate with human resources to define and clarify desired skills and experience.
- Use specific behaviorally based questions that help discover what each candidate has done and how the candidate approaches his or her work (the latter is often most important). If you are not skilled in interviewing techniques, then seek training or coaching, because this is necessary to make the right people decisions.
- Get to know the candidate's motivation for applying for this job. What does he or she want to get from the position? What work does he or she enjoy most? If it is a management position, make sure the candidate has a genuine interest in and capacity for management.
- Ask several people to interview each candidate. Ask each person to look for specific skills and qualities.

- When a candidate is applying from within the organization, talk with managers and others who have worked with the person and ask for their comments on whether he or she would be a good fit in the role for which the candidate is applying. Evaluate the results and his or her ability to execute.

- Conduct thorough reference checks! Many managers think reference checks are a waste of time, but this is not the case if they are done well. Even discussions with references provided by the candidate (presumably their allies) can be illuminating. References will often help break a tie between two strong candidates or confirm a nagging feeling about the person's background.

- If there are no candidates who are a great fit, keep looking. Do not settle for a person who is available and convenient. In the end, this will not benefit the organization or the person.

Middle managers who are picky about the people they bring onto their team will enjoy better results than their peers who are less selective. Each hiring decision communicates what you and the organization are looking for and the behaviors and skills that are most desirable. When the company hired Tim, an outstanding and energetic manager, the expectations for all managers got higher. By bringing Tim on, management had acknowledged that it valued proactive and creative managers, and in doing so had issued a subtle challenge to all other managers to show their best in these areas.

The high-impact middle management principles for optimizing individual performance work because they focus on the few actions that will lead to the greatest results. These five practices reinforce one another because they share three assumptions about performance. The first assumption is that most employees want to do a good job and make a positive difference. The second one is that ensuring employees are clear about expectations prevents and resolves many performance problems. And the third one is that employees want to work for well-managed and productive teams.

High-impact middle managers optimize performance by practicing the five performance principles consistently and methodically. They make sure that team members are clear about what is expected of them and how well they are currently performing, as compared with those expectations. The environment encourages and fosters intrinsic motivation by offering an inclusive and participative way for all team members to add value and make a difference. The team comprises highly talented folks who fit their roles and the team. High-impact middle managers know that doing these things is the 20 percent that will yield 80 percent (or the greatest benefit) toward optimizing individual performance.

Chapter 12

Coaching: Helping Others Achieve Breakthroughs

One of the quickest and most effective ways for a middle manager to make an impact on his or her organization is through coaching. Coaching yields short-term and long-term payoffs. Helping others achieve breakthroughs boosts results today and builds the organization's skills for tomorrow. Unfortunately, coaching is an underutilized and poorly understood middle management tool. Many managers confuse coaching with advice and counseling. Figure 12-1 shows the similarities and differences among these three forms of influence. In the figure, the areas where the circles intersect represent shared characteristics:

- The impetus for all three methods is to help the other person. Those who offer advice mean well, even though their opinions may be unwelcome.
- Both advice and counseling are directive and quick, but the receiver may welcome neither.
- Both advice and coaching address less urgent concerns and may consider the receiver's ideas.
- Both counseling and coaching focus on goals and may be effective for changing long-term behavior.

- Each method is useful in certain circumstances. Coaching is the only method of influence driven by the receiver, and it is the most valuable way to improve his or her effectiveness and success.

Coaching is different from advising, preaching, counseling, and persuading, because the last four are all done from the viewpoint of and for the person offering it. Coaching is the exact opposite. A great coach talks little, listens a lot, and facilitates the thinking process of the receiver. When coaching, the focus is on the receiver's goals and possibilities, not the receiver's performance.

Figure 12-1. Three Ways to Influence Others

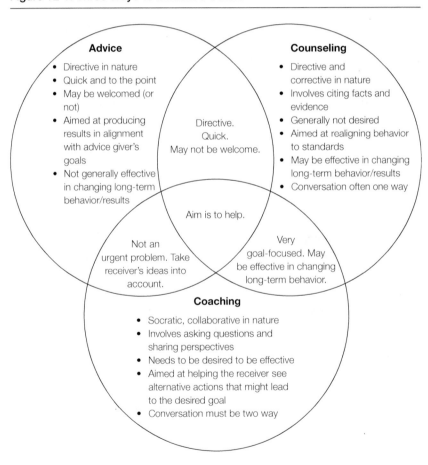

Coaches offer their time to help the progress of another. Coaches never try to replace the receiver's goals with their own (this would become advice or counseling). Though coaching is altruistic, it also benefits the middle managers who use it, because it improves results. It is important to recognize both the altruistic and selfish aspects of coaching, because doing so will help you choose coaching techniques that are most helpful to the receiver and the company.

Intrinsic motivation (see chapters 10 and 11) drives the best coaches to help others learn, grow, and perform. They get a charge out of helping people consider different viewpoints, and they enjoy seeing the proverbial light bulb turn on for them. Coaching can be one of the most fulfilling and meaningful roles for a middle manager. By helping others move their work forward, you broaden your reach within, and impact on, the organization.

Being a coach is rewarding—but not always easy. Sometimes the coach needs to be willing to discuss undiscussables or help uncover unwritten rules getting in the receiver's way. Receivers may perceive things in a way that is detrimental to their success. Coaches help them clarify what's real and what's not. A coach needs to be tough to hold the receiver accountable for realizing his or her goals. Doing this in a way that does not come across as bossy or directive can be tricky, but great coaches know that the secret lies in their intent to help, not control.

High-impact middle managers have a genuine interest in knowing how to help employees and peers be successful. They have learned techniques for facilitating helpful conversations. They know that coaching must be voluntary and welcomed by the receiver, not forced. Forced coaching becomes advice or feedback. Receivers should do most of the talking during coaching conversations. Great coaches ask many questions but otherwise let the receiver talk about his or her goals, ideas, and setbacks. They know that it is through this dialogue that the receiver is likely to see his or her challenge in a new and helpful way. Many people are comfortable with and welcome direction from their manager. Do not prescribe answers, because this will prevent learning from taking place. (You can, of course, help them learn where to go to get the answers!)

High-impact middle management coaching helps middle managers and receivers get the most out of coaching discussions. The elements of high-impact middle management coaching are

- ad hoc coaching
- formal coaching conversations
- coaching with the use of Socratic questions
- coaching infrastructures.

Let's look at each element.

Ad Hoc Coaching

Todd walked into Lou's office and asked for a few minutes to chat. Todd had an open position in his department, and he knew that it was going to be hard to fill. The tasks were so specific to the company that a current employee would best fill the job. Unfortunately, Todd could not think of a qualified internal candidate. Their conversation went like this:

LOU: What skills and behaviors are you looking for?

TODD: This position requires analytical skills, knowledge of the business, a proactive leadership presence, and—

LOU: Do they really need to be strong in all of these areas? Do other members of the team have experience in these areas?

TODD: The other team members are strong, yes, and they have worked for the company for a long time. So the new person does not need to have it all.

LOU: Which skills are the most important? What about filling this position concerns you most?

TODD: Above all else, I need someone who is a self-starter and who will take charge of the function. What I fear most is not being able to drive improvements fast enough.

LOU: If this is the case, why does the person need to come from inside the company?

TODD: I guess they don't, but I would prefer it.

LOU: OK, but keep challenging yourself on that assumption. Are there other positions that require similar skills and experiences?

TODD: There are a few I can think of.

LOU: Do any of the individuals in these positions have the behavioral qualities important for this job?

TODD: I'm not sure.

LOU: Are there employees in the operations group that have these skills?

TODD: I don't know. I would not have thought of them. Perhaps there are.

LOU: Do you know of any managers whose strengths may not be a match to their current position?

TODD: Yes, there are a few people like that... hmmm. Wait a minute; I've got it. Thanks. I will talk to you later!

Ad hoc coaching can occur anytime and in various ways. A breakthrough can occur while chatting in the hallway. High-impact middle managers seize opportunities to help their employees and peers. The dialogue between Todd and Lou is an example of ad hoc coaching. Middle managers practice ad hoc coaching when they take the initiative to ask questions that invigorate another person's thinking. Lou made it a habit to arrive a few minutes early to meetings. During this time, those around the table engaged in small talk and shared what was on the top of their minds. Lou had a knack for asking just the right question to help someone think about his or her problem in a new way. Lou would follow up with the employee after the meeting if it seemed that it would be helpful. Peers often shared their frustrations about projects they were struggling with, and Lou would offer to help them brainstorm and organize their thoughts.

Many managers think they coach more than they actually do. In reality, however, giving advice is a far more common practice than coaching. The primary distinction between ad hoc coaching and advice is the number of open-ended questions that typifies coaching. In addition, a good coach will resist the urge to tell people what they should do. Techniques for providing excellent ad hoc coaching include

- *Be available and accessible.* Ad hoc coaching can only occur if both parties have the time to talk. Middle managers who leave no time for informal discussions or who frequently close their office door will miss out on many opportunities to coach. Arrive at meetings a few minutes early, eat in the lunchroom, periodically have lunch with peers and employees, and stroll through the office several times a day.
- *Listen.* Employees and peers will share what is on their minds and highest on their list of challenges and concerns. Pick up on conversations in meetings and casual conversations.
- *Use Socratic questions to draw out new information and ideas* (see the examples later in this chapter). Express genuine interest and curiosity.
- *Facilitate action plans.* Receivers may have a difficult time putting their ideas and thoughts into an organized action plan. Coaches can help the receiver take action by making it easier for him or her to get started.
- *Encourage.* The receiver may be looking for someone to say, "Go for it!" Coaches encourage others to try new approaches and stretch boundaries.

Ad hoc coaching is a fantastic way for you to enable your team members to achieve results. Coaches who keep their eyes open and reserve their opinions will find ample opportunities to provide coaching and make a difference.

Formal Coaching Conversations

Ad hoc coaching works for many people and situations, but not all. Sometimes the best approach is to set aside time for a more formal coaching conversation. These formal conversations are most suitable for enabling large projects or personal goals to get off the ground. The primary reason for scheduling a formal session is to ensure that enough time is set aside to have a fruitful discussion. The conversation will be more effective when the coach and receiver embrace appropriate roles, as follows.

The coach:

- Asks the receiver to define his or her goal. What is he or she hoping to make happen?
- Keeps the discussion on track and moving.
- Asks questions that stimulate discussion (see the section on Socratic questions later in this chapter).
- Summarizes and clarifies discussion topics.
- Clarifies understanding of the receiver's goals and his or her motives for having those goals.
- Helps the receiver develop an action plan.
- Facilitates small victories for the receiver. For example, Lou knew that Denny wanted to learn more about other parts of the company and arranged for him to participate on a cross-functional project team. This assignment exposed him to several other functional groups and benefited the overall organization.

The coaching conversation progresses as the coach asks questions and makes statements that help to further the receiver's thinking. The goal for this discussion is for the receiver to expand his or her viewpoint, generate new approaches to meeting goals, and dispel assumptions or beliefs that are getting in the way of progress. The receiver may change his or her goals based on new insights or information. When done well, the receiver leaves the coaching session energized with new ideas and a clearer focus.

The receiver:

- Shares his or her goal, desired outcome, ideas, and motivations for the goal.
- Discusses questions, frustrations, and problems he or she has already faced.
- Shares the information that he or she has collected thus far.
- Defines his or her basic interpretations, judgments, assumptions, and points of view.

- Reviews the current progress he or she is making toward the goal and defines the barriers that are getting in the way.
- Is open to exploring new ideas and approaches.

Using Socratic Questions

Middle managers who use Socratic questions collect useful information that helps them coach and lead their functions. As coaches, middle managers can help their employees and peers develop critical thinking and creativity skills. Socratic questions enable coaches to facilitate conversations in a more effective way.

The Socratic method, named for the Greek philosopher Socrates, emphasizes the use of thought-provoking questions to promote learning (instead of offering opinions and advice) and challenges widely held beliefs.

Socratic questions are probing and open ended. You can use these questions in a business context to help others develop. The inquiry process is the cornerstone of this practice, because it helps receivers think creatively and solve problems using new approaches. Socratic questions also help the receiver clarify what he or she understands and what is yet unknown. Through this inquiry, strategies for improving effectiveness emerge while energizing the receiver's curiosity. Middle managers who use Socratic questions challenge the receiver in a way that is intrinsically motivating. Let's look at examples of Socratic questions.

Questions that clarify the receiver's goals:

- What would you like to have happen?
- How would you like to see this happen?
- Why are you favoring a change?
- What would you like to see change?
- If everything goes well, what will it look like in _____ months/ years?
- In your mind, what will happen if we do not change?

Questions that clarify the receiver's intent or motives:

- Why do you want this?
- Why do you say that?

- How would you benefit?
- Why is this important?
- What made you think of this?
- Who benefits from this?

Questions to ensure that the receiver's goals are aligned to get results:

- How does this relate to your goal or objective?
- Where do you think this goal will lead?
- What does this mean?
- What do we already know about . . . ?
- Why is this your goal?
- What do you think will happen?

Questions to uncover the receiver's basic assumptions:

- What basic assumptions do you have about this?
- Are there other assumptions that could also be valid?
- How do you know that what you believe is true?
- Do you agree with the following assumption: _____?
  Why? / Why not?
- What does _____think about this situation?
- What would happen if . . . ?
- What are the consequences of that assumption?
- Why do you think I asked this question?
- What is it about the question that is difficult to answer?

Questions to discover if the receiver has enough information:

- What do you need to know about this?
- What generalizations can you make?
- What data have you looked at already?
- How do you know that _____?
- Why do you think this is occurring?
- How can you be sure?
- Have you seen a situation like this before?
- What do you think is the cause?
- What evidence is there to support your assertion?

Questions to facilitate seeing other points of view:

- What would be an alternative?
- Is there another way to look at this? Why is it better?
- What are the pros and cons of this approach?
- How is this similar or different from what you have done in the past?
- What is the counterargument?
- What would someone who is against this idea say?
- What other ideas have you explored?
- How does this affect _____?

Socratic questions improve the coach's ability to remain objective by directing responses and conclusions back to the receiver. They also ask the receiver to consider many facets of a problem or goal, increasing the chances that new learning will occur.

Coaching Infrastructures

As a middle manager, you should think about how coaching can best be delivered in your organization. Some companies, like Verizon and Intel, have utilized formalized coaching structures. Coaches are trained, assigned, and expected to meet at regular and ad hoc times. Often, these coaching structures also document goals and one's progress in reaching them. Intel's mentoring program uses the company intranet to match partners (the learners) with potential mentors. Mentors and partners work toward goals stated in their mentoring contract. Meeting frequency and design are then left up to the mentor and partner.

Former CEO Raymond Smith described coaching at Bell Atlantic (now Verizon) as an important part of the management culture:

> Coaching is not seen as the least bit corny or unusual in our company. Once a week, one of us will ask, "Can I coach you on something?" In the past, I have never been able to do that comfortably. I was never able to do it without it being unnecessarily evasive on the one hand or unpleasant on the other. Now the

process is acceptable. It is group sanctioned. It's the way we've decided we're going to work together.

The pros of a formalized coaching structure include

- Coaching becomes part of the culture of the business.
- Assignment of coaches removes the stigma and embarrassment that some may associate with coaching.
- More people give and receive coaching under a formalized system.

The cons of a formalized coaching structure include

- Under a formalized coaching structure, the chances increase that people participate because it is compulsory or a corporate sacred cow. Mandatory systems often diminish some of the intrinsic motivation that can be associated with coaching.
- Formalized systems can be resource intensive and costly.
- Many formalized systems may not be flexible enough to meet the different needs of a diverse management group. It's hard to please all the people all of the time.

Many companies, like Mead Paper and Amazon.com, did not utilize formalized coaching structures during the time I worked with them. In these types of organizations, coaching was encouraged and supported, but there were no formal training or expectations. (Companies often say that managers should coach their employees, but most are not really talking about coaching as it has been defined here.) Most companies fall into this category. At Amazon.com, dynamic small team groups were utilized to encourage learning and development. Their formula was to hire diverse and smart people and let coaching and knowledge transfer happen by osmosis. This model can work if the environment is set up to encourage team problem solving and idea generation.

The pros of an informal coaching structure include

- Coaching tends to be timely and need based.
- Those who are excellent coaches will likely coach more than those who are poor coaches. In other words, the spontaneous

and personal nature of the system will lead to certain people being sought out to coach more than others are—a natural selection, of sorts, for coaching.

■ Coaching and being coached are likely to be more intrinsically motivating when they are not compulsory.

The cons of an informal coaching structure include

■ Fewer people receive coaching, and often the people who need it most do not seek out coaching.

■ Coaches are less likely to receive valuable training.

■ Without a structure to establish coaching as an important management tool, it is less likely to be valued and given a high priority.

In addition to formal and informal coaching structures, there are coaching models that fit along the spectrum between these two. There is no right or wrong method or approach to how coaching will be offered in an organization. As a middle manager, you are in the best position to assess and understand the best way to utilize coaching to develop people. Work with your peers, manager, and training department to ensure that the appropriate coaching model is evaluated and implemented. Why go to these lengths? Coaching, if done well, is one of your most powerful management tools. High-impact middle managers have learned that coaching and being coached is a high-value-added activity that enables you and your team members to achieve results.

Effective coaching helps you to maximize your impact. As a middle manager, you can help your staff achieve breakthroughs by recognizing and utilizing daily coaching opportunities. To be a great coach, it is first important to recognize what coaching is and what it is not. Giving someone your advice is not coaching. Whether you coach in an ad hoc or formal conversation, or as part of an established coaching structure, it is paramount that the coaching conversations be focused on and driven by the learner. By using these suggestions, you will improve your ability to coach peers and employees.

Part V

Honing Your Craft

Chapter 13

Coachability: How to Reach Goals Faster and Better

High-impact middle managers need to be highly coachable. What does being coachable mean? Much of a middle manager's day is concerned with guiding others, coaching team members, and assisting peers. However, it is just as important that middle managers ensure that they are getting the coaching, input, and development they need to be successful and continue to grow in their position. Coachability, then, is the degree to which you are open to what your environment can offer, or the extent to which you will accept and consider input and ideas.

High-impact middle managers know that their success depends on their being highly coachable when it counts most. Although all managers will be coachable some of the time and uncoachable during other moments, the most effective middle managers will be more coachable overall and, most important, during the times when it can make the greatest difference.

What Coachability Looks Like

Coachability is measured by how well a manager interacts with his or her environment; therefore, it is visible and observable behavior. Coachability is easy to recognize in others. When a manager is being coachable, there is an open, curious, and relaxed quality to his or her demeanor. When a manager is highly coachable, he or she

- is not defensive when challenged or offered an alternative view
- welcomes feedback and ideas for improvement
- asks for coaching
- considers and uses ideas offered by others
- seeks training and development in the form of reading, classes, new assignments, and coaching from others
- has a good sense of his or her strengths and weaknesses
- handles failures and setbacks with grace.

Being coachable usually goes hand in hand with confidence and a positive impression of one's own skills and abilities. Coachable managers display a sense of calm and a focus that allows them to take ideas and process them without feeling the need to defend or rationalize current methods. Highly coachable managers genuinely welcome and accept alternative points of view.

Middle managers who are uncoachable are also easy to identify. They put up barriers between themselves and others. Those who are uncoachable often look like this:

- They don't listen to ideas offered by others.
- They staunchly defend current ideas and approaches.
- They believe they must do things on their own and that asking for input is a sign of weakness.
- They appear to be unreceptive or not interested in coaching.
- They do not engage in conversations about development with their manager and view suggestions that they should develop new skills as criticism.
- They can be dismissive of others.

By observing how your peers behave during meetings and work sessions, you can begin to notice the behavioral cues that signal whether they are coachable or not. You should also seek to recognize these behaviors in yourself! Recognizing when you are being uncoachable is an important step toward improving your ability to accept constructive criticism.

Coachability Is a State of Mind

It is important to emphasize that people are not inherently coachable or uncoachable. Everyone has moments when they are coachable and others when they are not. Saying that someone is not a coachable person unfairly classifies him or her and does not recognize that coachability is a way of being that can be chosen at any given moment.

Middle managers interested in increasing their coachability need to examine what triggers their uncoachable moments. By understanding your personal triggers, you can recognize them and choose to be more coachable when the opportunity presents itself in the future. Here are examples of various emotional triggers:

- People triggered Harry's uncoachability when they questioned his decisions or opinions in front of his managers. He had a strong need to be right; and when challenged, he became uncoachable.
- Kathy refused to hear feedback if the idea suggested change or altered her tidy existence. She took great pride in planning her work; and when an idea had the potential to turn her world upside down, she resisted it, regardless of its merit or potential.
- Jim was often uncoachable when overwhelmed with too many tasks. His peers and managers eventually learned that it was best to save ideas or suggestions for another day if Jim had a backlog of projects or meetings.
- Corky was coachable when talking with others in her field of expertise but quickly became defensive about suggestions offered from individuals outside her department.

All middle managers encounter circumstances or people that trigger their uncoachability. Understanding and recognizing the obstacles that get in the way of your coachability is the first step toward becoming more receptive and, therefore, more successful. For example, a trigger for uncoachability may be something as simple as the time of day. You may find that you, or a peer, are not receptive to coaching at the end of a busy day that has been filled with meetings and projects. If you are sensitive about getting feedback or constructive criticism, you may prefer to schedule coaching sessions early in the morning before the majority of staff arrives or after most people have left the office and you are free of distractions. The size and composition of the group might also make a difference in how open you are to coaching. Do you prefer coaching sessions to be one-to-one, or with immediate peers? Are you less receptive to coaching if senior managers are present?

Even high-impact middle managers are human. It is important for you to be aware of your mood and recognize when you are not feeling coachable. It is better to reschedule a conversation or meeting for another time than to be uncoachable and get little from the conversation. Once you become aware of your triggers and resistance points, you can open yourself up to more opportunities for improvement and perhaps a break-through.

Coachability as a Definition of Success

High-impact middle managers strive to be extremely teachable. They adopt the belief that being highly coachable is important if they are to be successful. Coachable managers have altered their definition of what respect and competence look like. They know that they will be well re-garded and held in higher esteem if they openly accept ideas and sugges-tions from others.

How does Dell Computer Corporation, for instance, encourage coachability? Given that survival in the high-technology field is incum-bent upon staying ahead of the knowledge curve, Michael Dell, the firm's CEO, cites coachability as a key requirement for himself, as well as the managers in his company. In his best-selling book *Direct from Dell: Strategies That Revolutionized an Industry*, he had this to say about learning:

> Our people are obviously motivated by the ways we link our goals to their compensation and incentives. But more impor-tantly, there are ways in which we work to instill ownership thinking in our people and better leverage their talents so they can reach their full potential. The willingness and ability to learn constantly is one of them.... I approach learning from

the standpoint of asking questions: What would make your job at Dell easier? What do our customers like and not like? What would they like to see us doing better? How can we improve? I start by asking a lot of questions and doing a lot of listening: You don't learn anything when you're talking.

Stimulating, open, and meaningful conversations encourage coachability and learning. Middle managers who employ Dell's method of asking numerous open-ended questions will find that the coachability of others improves. The discussions that come out of such a dialogue will yield creative and useful ideas.

High-impact middle managers know that they will be much more successful if they focus on getting the best results, which will come from hearing and using the advice of many, rather than from being right. They regularly ask for input and coaching from many different people.

Techniques for Improving Your Coachability

In addition to recognizing when you are being coachable or uncoachable and embracing the belief that being coachable is important for success, there are several specific techniques you can use to improve your coachability. These methods will also help high-impact middle managers improve their ability to solve problems and generate creative opportunities. They include the following:

- *Coachability starts with a mindset.* When you notice that you are being uncoachable, pause, take a deep breath, and decide to let go of the feelings of resistance and be more open.
- *Ask more open-ended questions to glean more information about projects and processes.*
- *Ask follow-up questions to understand ideas and suggestions fully.*
- *Take the initiative to ask for input on one problem, idea, or topic each day.*
- *Resist the urge to defend yourself or say why an idea won't work.* Focus on the desired outcome, not on being right.
- *Schedule brainstorming and problem-solving meetings during the time of day or week that you are most coachable.*

These techniques can help you immediately improve your overall coachability and ensure that you are being coachable when it matters most. High-impact middle managers have developed the ability to monitor their coachability and quickly choose behaviors that support that. They have learned that becoming more coachable is a test of mind over matter that gets easier with practice and experience.

Using Coachability to Attract a Breakthrough

Breakthroughs happen when people let them. Sometimes middle managers are like sponges, happily soaking in new information. All too often, however, preconceived notions, fears, and the ego shut out the opportunities that these managers seek. Coachability is the level of openness a manager has toward outside influences and development. There is a strong positive relationship between breakthroughs and a high level of coachability. Middle managers who want to experience breakthrough results can improve their odds by carefully preparing their work environment and themselves. To attract a breakthrough, try these 10 methods:

1. *Let peers, managers, and employees know about the most important or interesting topics or challenges that you are working on.* The more people are enrolled in a challenge, the better the chances that a terrific idea or approach will surface.

2. *Call a meeting to brainstorm ideas and suggestions.* Encourage diverse points of view and a variety of ideas. Go beyond inviting the most logical choices of people to the meeting and include those who have had great ideas about other problems.

3. *Seek nontraditional avenues of information and ideas.* Read current research and periodicals related to this topic.

4. *Don't be shy.* Call or email top thinkers and researchers in the field and ask for their perspectives.

5. *Focus on defining the ideal desired outcome and asking questions about what conditions would need to exist to support this outcome.*

6. *Take, and be fully engaged in, a course on the subject.*

7. *Make a request that you would normally consider unreasonable.* It generally does not hurt to ask, and may even work! Most middle managers

are so conservative about what they ask for that their unreasonable requests are not likely to be that unreasonable.

8. *Adopt a "this shall be" mindset.* There seems to be some legitimacy to the self-fulfilling prophecy (when an expectation appears to lead to or cause the anticipated outcome), so managers might as well have this phenomenon work in their favor.

9. *If important enough, ask an outside facilitator to lead a group of people through a work session to brainstorm ideas, approaches, barriers, and desired outcomes.* Professional facilitators can often detect the dynamics of the group and guide the discussion for the best outcome.

10. *Benchmark other admired and respected companies that perform this particular task or process extremely well.*

Breakthroughs are improvements that lead to a significant change. This change can be physically tangible, such as a new process or product, or in your mind, such as a new way of looking at an old problem. Either way, you can increase your odds of experiencing a breakthrough by taking the initiative to establish an environment that will support breakthrough thinking.

Coachability Opens Doors

Middle managers who increase their number of coachable moments will find the door of opportunity opens wide. Possibilities never thought possible become real, and obstacles fall by the wayside. Highly coachable middle managers are also highly promotable! Senior managers respect and value managers who do whatever it takes to produce the best results. Coachable managers will get more done and will utilize and implement more creative solutions than their peers who are less coachable.

Some middle managers do not value coachability because they believe that they need to appear strong and confident. Do not confuse confidence with ego. High-impact middle managers are strong, confident leaders—and they are highly coachable. When middle managers can demonstrate both confidence and coachability, they improve their ability to get results through cooperation with other people and enjoy a successful career with many new and interesting challenges.

Coachability is an important qualification for high-impact middle managers. Middle managers need to be coachable to meet the diverse and challenging requirements of their jobs. By recognizing what coachability looks like and by employing techniques that enhance your coachability, you can improve your results and effectiveness. Being coachable is having a very engaged and interested state of mind—a feeling many find intrinsically motivating. Moving fast in the right direction feels great. Increased success and respect are great tonics that will reinforce the benefits of being coachable.

Chapter 14

The High-Impact Middle Management System: Putting It Together for Maximum Managerial Flow

As was described on the first page of the introduction, high-impact middle management has a rhythm, or a flow, that can be intensely satisfying and successful. In his book *Beyond Boredom and Anxiety*, Mihaly Csikszentmihalyi described the flow experience as one where moments flow in a unified, focused, and intrinsically stimulating manner. High-impact middle managers often experience flow at work. They are talented, prepared, and energized to make things happen. They have internalized their role and the beliefs that will serve them best. These managers have tried and now habitually practice most of the techniques presented in this book.

Reread the first two paragraphs of the introduction. Here they are again:

> In any organization, there are two kinds of middle managers. There are those who get the work done but never think beyond what needs to be completed in the short term. They rush from one task to another, never quite recognizing which is most important to their company's larger objectives. Though they may work hard and have good intentions, they fail to see the big picture and, thus, add little value to their organization or the functions

they manage. Then there are high-impact middle managers. These managers see the big picture. They know how to manage operational practices and execute tactical goals to support strategic initiatives. They add value to their organization and thus elevate their position from that of an intermediary to key player.

There is an almost magical synergy in a work environment when high-impact middle managers operate at peak efficiency. Their questions are timely and on target; their ideas are provocative in ways that help move the work forward. They know how to think strategically. Transitions from one task to the next seem choreographed. As they walk through the office, their demeanor is calm but they have a sense of urgency. Busy, focused, and driven, these managers produce results and imbue the workplace with energy. Those who watch these managers may feel motivated or intimidated—but they are not unaffected.

Have you ever had a day like that? If you have, you undoubtedly know that it is something that you don't think about as it is occurring—it just happens. When at the top of your game, you are not likely to think about what you are doing or how you are doing it. Middle managers who internalize the High-Impact Middle Management System in their own way and style will enjoy the flow experience more often than many of their peers. Why? High-impact middle management is designed with several important elements of flow in mind—including fun, challenge, excitement, contribution, and focus. Sound familiar? These are also common intrinsic motivators.

To produce maximum managerial flow, you will want to ensure that you love your job and are feeling the sense of accomplishment and satisfaction that comes with having an impact and making a difference. You will want to have fun with your work! So please use these techniques in the way that works best for you.

You likely have noticed that there are two types of suggestions offered in this book. First and foremost, there are beliefs, mindsets, and ways of thinking. Second, the system offers pragmatic tools and practices suggested by the high-impact middle management belief set—or definition of success. To begin internalizing the system, take on some of the beliefs and try them. Often, the techniques will easily follow from holding these beliefs.

Where should you begin? The most important suggestion for how to get started is to get started! Getting into action and trying the High-Impact Middle Management System is more important than how you do it or with which technique you begin. Because the system elements support and reinforce one another, it does not matter where you start. Just start.

Keeping the High-Impact Middle Management System Top of Mind: The Scorecard

Regularly reviewing the beliefs and practices will help you internalize the system. As presented in chapters 2 and 5, clarifying goals and communicating them to others improves performance. Middle managers who clarify their personal management development goals and refer to them often will outperform managers who set and then forget about goals. The High-Impact Middle Management Scorecard is a synopsis of the system's elements and techniques; see figure 14-1.

How to Use the Scorecard
Middle managers can begin to put these methods and tools to work for them by reviewing the scorecard at the beginning of each day. In time, application of the summarized gems found on the scorecard will become second nature. This will enable the middle manager to access the tools more readily, recognize opportunities for putting high-impact middle management to work for him or her, and encourage the flow experience.

Using the ROR Cheat Sheet as a Tool for Breakthroughs
On the back of the scorecard is a reprint of the results-oriented responses, or RORs, as presented in chapter 1. This ROR Cheat Sheet can help middle managers diagnose potential response problems and opportunities for specific problem areas such as a project that has stalled or a problem that won't go away.

Figure 14-1. High-Impact Middle Management Scorecard

High-Impact Middle Management Principles

- Being a middle manager is exciting.
- Middle management is a craft.
- Great managers do what others don't.
- Beliefs determine behavior.
- Relationships influence results.
- Strengths and weaknesses are known.
- Middle management can be learned, but one must "get it."
- Middle managers exist to make things happen.

**Remember the 80/20 rule.
Do the 20% that gets you the 80%.**

Organization Alignment

- Clarify the vision, purpose, and goals for the department.
- Use blank tablet creativity.
- Compare the needs of the department, the ideal plan, and current roles and processes.
- Generate organization optimization alternatives.
- Realign structure, processes, and procedures.
- Measure and monitor processes and workflow.

Use Socratic questions!

Power Partnership Techniques

- Make it a priority and expectation to be a great partner.
- Resist the need to control.
- Spend time with peers.
- Resolve any past partnership failures.
- Communicate well with and on behalf of peers.
- If you cannot say anything nice, do not say anything at all.
- Take ownership of problems and challenges.
- Be coachable and easy to work with.
- Graciously share credit.
- Know the needs and concerns of peers, managers, customers, and employees.

High-Impact Middle Management Definition of Success

- Middle managers are expected to be accountable and take ownership.
- Middle managers are expected to make a positive contribution to the business.
- Middle managers should be outstanding role models.
- Middle managers need to execute and get results.
- Developing and maintaining productive business relationships are important.
- Flexible and nimble teams are more successful.
- Being a middle manager is a great and important job.
- Success means making the greatest possible difference, delivering results, and managing people for optimal productivity and satisfaction.
- Looking good means being regarded open and coachable.

Navigating through Mucky-Muck

- Lighten up and roll with it.
- Do the right homework.
- Pick the battles to fight and those to let go.
- Focus energy where it will count.
- Overcommunicate, be inclusive, follow up.
- Analyze and fix it.
- Ask probing questions.
- Repair relationships.
- Believe in people's capacity for change and learning.
- See and enjoy accomplishments.
- Get organized.

Don't be a mucky muck generator.

Ad Hoc Coaching

- Be available and accessible.
- Listen.
- Use Socratic questions.
- Have fun with coaching.
- Facilitate action plans.
- Encourage others.

Mastering Time

- Perform periodic time audits.
- Set the pace.
- Apply the 80/20 rule to choices about time.
- Use tiny pockets of time to get big results.
- Plan, plan, plan.

Be highly coachable!

Use the High-Impact Middle Management Playbook to improve work planning and execution!

What to Measure

- Most important contribution
- Customer expectations
- Primary products and services
- Throughput
- Team goals
- Major initiatives/projects

Good Reputation

- Can be trusted.
- Does what he or she promises.
- Produces good results.
- Is pleasurable or easy to work with.
- Is knowledgeable and creative in his or her chosen field.
- Is an asset to the company.

Throughput Problems

- Bottlenecks
- Constraints
- Slow process connections
- Lengthy critical paths
- Skills deficiencies
- Mucky-muck

To Optimize Performance

- Ensure that everyone knows what he or she is expected to achieve.
- Have regular conversations about how each employee is doing.
- Do #1 and #2 in ways that maximize intrinsic motivation.
- Take decisive and proactive action to deal with poor performers.
- Be very picky when hiring. Do not settle.

Attracting a Breakthrough

- Let peers, managers, and employees know the topics or challenges of greatest interest and importance.
- Brainstorm ideas and suggestions.
- Seek nontraditional avenues of information.
- Don't be shy.
- Focus on defining the ideal desired outcome and asking questions.
- Take, and be fully engaged in, a class on the subject.
- Make unreasonable requests.
- Adopt a "this shall be" mindset.
- Ask an outside facilitator to lead a work session.
- Benchmark others.

The ROR Cheat Sheet works by prompting you to think about how you have been approaching a particular problem and will offer potential alternative approaches. Teams can use the cheat sheet to help them solve problems and implement improvements. The cheat sheet is also a good reference for staff or planning meetings.

Conclusion: It Is Just the Beginning!

Honing one's craft is a satisfying and fruitful endeavor. It takes time, commitment, and a passion for the work. Each new idea, skill, method, experience, and tool adds to the high-impact middle manager's knowledge bank and allows the middle manager to develop his or her own brand of management. Middle management growth and development is a rich and tailored process that provides organizations with the diverse and creative talent they need to prosper. The objective of the High-Impact Middle Management System is to add to your cache of methods for dealing with complexity, setbacks, and possibilities. Of course, each middle manager will interpret this book differently and take different things from it.

Some may strive for sameness, but differences are what energize the field of management. Whereas diversity of thought, action, and approach benefits organizations, there are basic propositions that underlie the individual approaches of the most successful middle managers—those referred to here as high-impact middle managers. These propositions are presented and reinforced throughout this book. Therefore, while you should follow your individual path for using the techniques, keep these things in mind:

- High-impact middle managers are driven to make things better. They know that their roles exist to move work forward in ways that would not occur without them.
- Successful middle managers are proactive. There is simply too much going on every day, and reactive managers cannot accomplish the needed work.
- High-impact middle managers know they are important and make a difference. They take their roles seriously and possess

professionalism commensurate with these roles. They know they are role models and the perpetuators of corporate culture.

- High-impact middle managers believe that the most important work they do is management. They measure accomplishment in terms of management successes in addition to numbers of widgets produced.

- Managers don't control people, and control-oriented performance management approaches can never maximize individual performance. High-impact middle managers have learned to temper their need to control people and instead focus on controlling their own behaviors, as well as departmental processes and systems.

- Employees, peers, and managers want their middle managers to be at their best and to continue developing new skills. Conventional thinking might lead managers to believe that as they move up the corporate food chain, they have less to learn and do not need as much coaching. High-impact middle managers have figured out that this is not true. To provide the value and contribution the organization and team members seek, middle managers need to learn more and receive more coaching than they did while they were frontline supervisors. The middle manager's job is different, and the scope of responsibility is immense.

- High-impact middle managers know that one of the most important choices they make each day is how to spend their limited time.

These themes are common among the best middle managers and run throughout the High-Impact Middle Management System. They are embedded in the guiding principles and can be found as elements of the dozens of techniques and tools offered here. High-impact middle managers have figured out what they need to do to maximize short-term and long-term results, and they do these things. Their work is successful and fruitful. High-impact middle managers cover a lot of ground in their organizations. Therefore, the middle manager's breadth of responsibility is significant, and the best have learned how to have an impact on results across the organization. Senior executives expect their middle managers to influence every level of the company, and high-impact middle management will help middle managers effectively reach the people and processes that need their attention and guidance.

This book seeks to reveal the compelling and intriguing elements of the middle manager's job, so that current middle managers will appreciate the work they do, and those not currently in the field will want in. Professionals interested in making a significant contribution to their organization and gaining great satisfaction from their work know that being a middle manager can provide these rewards.

Please use this book often and as a reference. Good luck as you hone your middle management craft. Enjoy the path and the destination, for the ride can be just as invigorating as the finish. Here's to experiencing the magic and flow of high-impact middle management!

You are all superheroes to me.

Appendix:
Recommended Reading and Online Resources
for Middle Managers

Recommended Reading

Abolishing Performance Appraisals: Why They Backfire and What to Do Instead, by Tom Coens and Mary Jenkins. Berrett Koehler.

Beyond Boredom and Anxiety, by Mihaly Csikszentmihalyi. Jossey-Bass.

Circle of Innovation, by Tom Peters. Alfred A. Knopf.

Control Your Destiny or Someone Else Will: Lessons in Mastering Change, by Noel M. Tichy and Stratford Sherman. HarperInformation.

Critical Chain, by Eliyahu M. Goldratt. North River Press.

Deming and Goldratt: The Theory of Constraints and the System of Profound Knowledge, by Domenico Lepore and Oded Cohen. North River Press.

Direct from Dell: Strategies That Revolutionized an Industry, by Michael Dell with Catherine Fredman. HarperBusiness.

The Empowered Manager: Positive Political Skills at Work, by Peter Block. Jossey-Bass.

The Essential Drucker: The Best of Sixty Years of Peter Drucker's Essential Writings on Management, by Peter Drucker. HarperBusiness.

Execution: The Discipline of Getting Things Done, by Larry Bossidy, Ram Charan, and Charles Burck. Crown Publishing Group.

The Fifth Discipline, by Peter Senge. Currency.

Flight of the Buffalo: Soaring to Excellence, Learning to Let Employees Lead, by Ralph Stayer and James Belasco. Warner Books.

The Goal: A Process of Ongoing Improvement, by Eliyahu M. Goldratt and Jeff Cox. North River Press.

Good to Great: Why Some Companies Make the Leap . . . and Others Don't, by Jim Collins. HarperCollins.

How to Win Friends and Influence People, by Dale Carnegie, Dorothy Carnegie, and Arthur R. Pell. Pocket Books.

Implementing Your Strategic Plan: How to Turn "Intent" into Effective Action for Sustainable Change, by C. Davis Fogg. Amacom.

It's Not Luck, by Eliyahu Goldratt. North River Press.

It's Your Ship: Management Techniques from the Best Damn Ship in the Navy, by Captain D. Michael Abrashoff. Warner Books.

Learning Organizations: Developing Cultures for Tomorrow's Workplace, edited by Sarita Chawla and John Renesch. Productivity Press.

Management: Tasks, Responsibilities, Practices, by Peter Drucker. Harper.

Managing Transitions: Making the Most of Changes, by William Bridges. Addison-Wesley.

Masterful Coaching: Extraordinary Results, by Impacting People and the Way They Think and Work Together, by Robert Hargrove. Jossey-Bass.

Maverick: The Success Story Behind the World's Most Unusual Workplace, by Ricardo Semler. Warner Books.

No Contest: The Case Against Competition, by Alfie Kohn. Houghton Mifflin.

Nuts! Southwest Airlines' Crazy Recipe for Business and Personal Success, by Kevin Freiberg and Jackie Freiberg. Bard Press.

The 100 Best Business Books of All Time, by Jack Covert and Todd Sattersten. Portfolio.

Outliers, by Malcolm Gladwell. Little, Brown and Company.

Out of the Crisis, by W. Edwards Deming. MIT Press.

Punished by Rewards: The Trouble with Gold Stars, Incentive Plans, A's, Praise, and Other Bribes, by Alfie Kohn. Houghton Mifflin.

Reengineering Management: The Mandate for New Leadership, by James Champy. HarperBusiness.

Reengineering the Corporation: A Manifesto for Business Revolution, by Michael Hammer and James Champy. HarperBusiness.

Secrets of Executive Success: How Anyone Can Handle the Human Side of Work and Grow Their Career, by Mark Golin, Mark Bricklin, Dave Diamond and the Rodale Center for Executive Development. Rodale Press.

Seven Habits Of Highly Effective People, by Stephen R. Covey. Simon & Schuster.

Skilled Facilitator: Practical Wisdom for Developing Effective Groups, by Roger Schwarz. Jossey-Bass.

The Social Construction of Reality: A Treatise in the Sociology of Knowledge, by Peter L. Berger and Thomas Luckman. Anchor Books.

Stewardship: Choosing Service or Self-Interest, by Peter Block. Berrett Kohler.

Talent Is Overrated, by Geoff Colvin. Portfolio.

Topgrading: How Leading Companies Win by Hiring, Coaching, and Keeping the Best People, by Bradford D. Smart. Prentice Hall.

Tribes, by Seth Godin. Portfolio.

What the CEO Wants You to Know: How Your Company Really Works, by Ram Charan. Crown Publishing Group.

Online Resources

See Lisa Haneberg's company website, www.managementperformance.com, and her personal website, www.lisahaneberg.com. Also check out her blog, Management Craft, at www.managementcraft.com.

Great Weblogs (Blogs)

800-CEO-READ Blog, http://800ceoread.com/blog/

Agile Management Blog, www.agilemanagement.net/Articles/Weblog/blog.html

Cranky Middle Manager, www.crankymiddlemanager.com

Employee Engagement Zingers, www.davidzinger.com/

Fast Company's blog, www.fastcompany.com/

Genuine Curiosity, www.genuinecuriosity.com/genuinecuriosity/

HR Capitalist, www.hrcapitalist.com/

Johnnie Moore, www.johnniemoore.com/blog/

Life Beyond Code, www.lifebeyondcode.com/

Management Issues, www.management-issues.com/default.asp

Management Skills, www.managementblog.org/

Manager Tools, www.manager-tools.com/

Phil Gerbyshak, www.philgerbyshak.com/

Presentation Zen, www.presentationzen.com/presentationzen/

Ramblings from a Glass Half Full, www.terrystarbucker.com/

Seth Godin, http://sethgodin.typepad.com/seths_blog/

Slacker Manager, www.bizzia.com/slackermanager/

Slow Leadership, www.slowleadership.org/blog/

Talking Story with Say Leadership Coaching, www.sayleadershipcoaching.com/talkingstory/

Three Star Leadership, http://blog.threestarleadership.com/

You Already Know This Stuff, http://youalreadyknowthisstuff.blogspot.com/

Other Websites

www.hbr.com: *Harvard Business Review* online. Download and purchase articles on almost any management or leadership topic.

www.fortune.com: Online home of *Fortune* magazine. Always interesting and allows for searching of old articles.

www.fastcompany.com: Website for *Fast Company* magazine, which is one of the more creative and innovative business magazines available to middle managers.

http://800ceoread.com/: A terrific place to find information about business books.

www.tompeters.com: Tom Peters's website always has lots of interesting information. He is still thought provoking after all these years!

www.pfdf.org: Peter F. Drucker Foundation for Nonprofit Management.

www.businessweek.com: *BusinessWeek* online magazine.

online.wsj.com: *The Wall Street Journal* online.

www.business2.com: *Business 2.0* online magazine.

About the Author

Lisa Haneberg is vice president and organizational development practice leader for MPI Consulting and has taught and coached hundreds of managers during the past 25 years—including hotel managers, power tool manufacturing department leaders, paper mill union presidents, microchip fabrication shift managers, distribution center leaders, ship captains, division vice presidents, and corporate presidents. Each has benefited from the straightforward solutions to common management maladies that she offers. As a manager, management trainer, and coach for companies both large and small, she has held leadership positions focused on manager development and effectiveness. Her expertise includes one-to-one management coaching, management course facilitation, organization development, and business writing. She is a certified master trainer and behavioral assessment interpreter. Management is her passion. She is an avid speaker, trainer, and blogger. Find her online at www.managementcraft.com and www.lisahaneberg.com. Her other books include *Organization Development Basics* (ASTD Press, 2005); *Coaching Basics* (ASTD Press, 2006); *Focus Like a Laser Beam: 10 Ways to Do What Matters Most* (Jossey Bass, 2006); *Two Weeks to a Breakthrough: How to Zoom toward Your Goal in 14 Days or Less* (Jossey Bass, 2007); *10 Steps to Be a Successful Manager* (ASTD Press, 2007); *Developing Great Managers: 20 Power Hours* (ASTD Press, 2008); and *Hip and Sage: Staying Smart, Cool and Competitive in the Workplace* (Davies Black and ASTD Press, 2009).

Tell Me What You Think

I would like your feedback! The High-Impact Middle Management System has been a labor of love developed over the last 20 years. It will continue to expand and improve over time and as new techniques are tested and proved to be effective. Please drop me an email message at lhaneberg@gmail.com. Your opinions are important and valued. Thank you for your feedback!

Index